WOMEN
ASTRONAUTS
Aboard the Shuttle

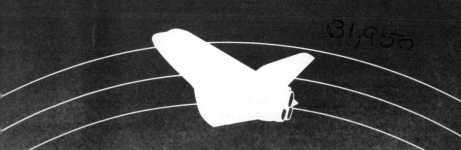

$13,95$

WOMEN ASTRONAUTS
Aboard the Shuttle

MARY VIRGINIA FOX

Julian Messner   New York

Copyright © 1984 by Mary Virginia Fox

All rights reserved including the right of
reproduction in whole or in part in any form.
Published by Julian Messner,
A Division of Simon & Schuster, Inc.
Simon & Schuster Building,
1230 Avenue of the Americas,
New York, New York 10020.

JULIAN MESSNER and colophon are trademarks of
Simon & Schuster, Inc.
All photos courtesy of NASA.

10 9 8 7 6 5 4 3 2 1

Manufactured in the United States of America

Design by A Good Thing, Inc.

Library of Congress Cataloging in Publication Data.

Fox, Mary Virginia.
    Women astronauts.

    Bibliography: p.
    Includes index.
    Summary: Describes the June, 1983 flight of the space
shuttle with emphasis on the experiences of Sally Ride,
the first American woman to fly in space. Also includes
brief biographies of the eight women astronauts
discussing their training and their future participation
in space flights.
    1. Space shuttles—Juvenile literature. 2. Women
astronauts—United States—Juvenile literature.
[1. Space shuttles. 2. Women astronauts] I. Title.
TL795.F69   1984   629.45′0092′2 [B]   84-1126
ISBN 0-671-53105-0

CONTENTS

1	Blastoff	7
2	Floating Free	18
3	Satellite Away	24
4	"We Pick Up and Deliver"	30
5	Weather Glitch	39
6	Sally Ride	47
7	Judith Resnik	57
8	Margaret Rhea Seddon	63
9	Shannon Lucid	69
10	Kathryn Sullivan	79
11	Anna Fisher	85
12	Mary Cleave	91
13	Bonnie Dunbar	103
14	Astronaut Candidates	109
15	Simulating the Mission	119
16	Survival Training	123
17	Suiting Up	137
18	Where They Hang the Bird	143
19	Whose Turn Next?	150
	Suggested Further Readings	156
	Index	157

The STS-7 crew speaking to the press at the Shuttle Landing Facility at the Kennedy Space Center a few days before the launch of the **Challenger**.

Astronauts Robert L. Crippen, crew commander; John Fabian, mission specialist; Frederick Hauck, pilot; and Sally Ride, mission specialist. Four-fifths of the STS-7 crew take a break from simulations a month before liftoff.

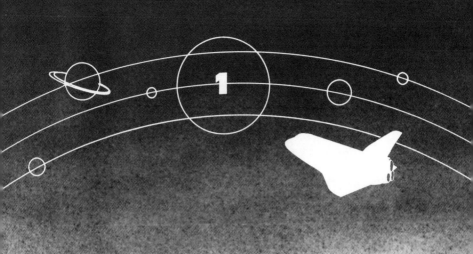

BLASTOFF

June 18, 1983.

There were knocks on five very important doors at the Cape in Florida that morning. It was time to eat breakfast, not that appetites always correspond to schedules, but it would be the last time for at least six days that Shuttle Commander Robert Crippen, pilot Rick Hauck, mission specialists John Fabian and Sally Ride, and medical doctor Norman Thagard would be able to enjoy earthly food.

The press had been alerted. The breakfast hour was not to be a private affair. Every bite was to be recorded on film. It was noted that all five astronauts wore matching navy and white tee shirts. The public wanted to know all the details.

Again Sally Ride was the center of attention. She was tanned, curly headed, with an excited grin, but undoubtedly she was wishing this tedious hour with the press was over so that the important business of the day could begin.

As First American Woman in Space, her life had suddenly become public property. She had pointed out that in the past 22 years 57 men had traveled in outer space, but no one listened.

"It may be too bad that our society isn't further along, and that this is such a big deal," she said. But it was a big deal, and with it she carried an added load of responsibility. How she handled herself would affect the other seven women astronauts now in training.

She got through the breakfast hour admirably. Now it was time for one last perfunctory check of blood pressure and pulse by a NASA nurse. Then a change of clothing to the blue pants and jacket with the STS-7 (STS-7 = Space Transportation System—Flight 7) patch on the pocket, designed especially for this flight. No clumsy pressurized space suits for this Shuttle, except for scheduled space walks.

Pleats have been stitched into the uniforms with elasticized thread to accommodate the changing dimensions and posture of the astronauts during

Ride responding to a question from an interviewer.

flight. In near-zero gravity they will grow an inch or two because the discs between the vertebrae of their backs will no longer be pushed down by gravity. Fluids in the lower parts of their bodies will flow upward. Waists will soon be smaller, legs skinnier. All of this will only be temporary.

Now the astronauts are ready to be bussed to the launch pad. Already the "hand-over" team has been aboard the Shuttle. This is the group of technicians who have spent the last day and a half checking every system, every gauge, every computer to make sure everything is in order. Nothing is left to chance or to one person.

Exactly two hours before the scheduled liftoff time of 7:33 A.M. EST, the official astronaut van arrives at the base of the launch pad. It is still a gray dawn, but floodlights illuminate the huge bird, giving it an unearthly glow.

The piece of machinery they are all so familiar with is still an awesome sight. Its tail section in flight is the height of an eight-story building. Now its nose is pointed straight toward the sky. The three bell-shaped engines are the most advanced liquid fuel engines ever built. They have to be powerful to lift 4.4 million pounds into space.

The Shuttle's stubby wings are swept far back from the cockpit. Two long pencil-shaped rockets on either side of the craft provide most of the power to lift the Shuttle off the pad and propel it during the first two minutes of flight. When their job is done, the rockets descend by parachute and are later retrieved by salvage ships.

Only the big belly tank will burn up in the atmosphere after it is empty. The tank is a raw amber color. Someone reasoned correctly that it was just a waste of paint and money to make it a sparkling white match of the rest of the craft, and that paint would have added an unnecessary six hundred pounds of weight.

The astronauts enter the elevator that takes them up the 374-foot-high scaffold, or gantry, that holds the Shuttle in its launch position. This is their closest look at the strange jigsaw-puzzle surface of their home for the next six days. The entire body of the craft is covered with porous cinder-like tiles of insulation, 32,000 of them, no two exactly alike. The aluminum shell of the spacecraft is constantly flexing and bending so that it could not be coated without seams.

The elevator stops at the cockpit level. They are greeted by another team of workers who dust off their shoes and help them adjust their Snoopy Hats. Those familiar helmets with earphones and communication hook-up are worn during liftoff and landing. This is the only part of their gear that makes them look like space-age travelers.

They crawl through a circular hatch that is only 40 inches in diameter. Actually there are three levels to this forward section. The pilot's and commander's stations are somewhat like the cockpit of a 747. Control panels line the space below and above the windows and on the ceiling. The panels are studded with what look like a thousand beer can openers. Each tab is a switch. Buttons are not used. It is too easy to accidentally activate a button by bumping into it when drifting around in zero gravity.

Each switch controls some essential function of the spacecraft. A mission specialist must know each one as well as the pilot. The reason there are so many controls is that there are three for every function. If, for example, an electrical system fails, a second one takes over, and if this too should malfunction, there is a third back-up system.

The middle deck where they enter is the living section. On the ground, accommodations seem unbelievably crowded, but that's only for a few minutes in flight. Without gravity, walls and ceilings become floors. Chairs can be stowed away in the lowest storage section. The astronauts soon will be able to float easily between decks without a ladder.

Sally Ride crawls forward and up a ladder to find her seat behind the pilot. The astronauts settle themselves in their reclining chairs. Actually they are lying on their backs in a seated position with their feet above their heads. This helps them withstand the acceleration during liftoff. Astronauts on earlier flights of Apollo, Gemini, and Mercury rockets had to endure 8.1 "g's" of force that jammed their bodies hard against their contoured chairs during blastoff. A "g" is the weight of pull of Earth's gravity on your body at sea level. So an 8.1 "g" force would be 8.1 times what you would feel normally.

Sally Ride and her team will be much more comfortable on this flight. They won't feel a pull of more than 3 "g's," just what you might expect going around a corner at a very fast speed.

They are now strapped in, waiting for that awesome moment. Dr. Ride has been assigned the job of flight engineer. She will be monitoring the workings of the spacecraft. She will be calling them off to the pilot and commander, who in turn are going through their own check list of measurements. The countdown proceeds exactly on schedule.

Actually the countdown has been going on for almost a year, from the day the crew was announced, and before that, when the purpose of the mission was planned. There have been hours, days,

Ride dons a helmet and straps herself into a seat in the Shuttle Mission Simulator a few weeks before the **Challenger** flight.

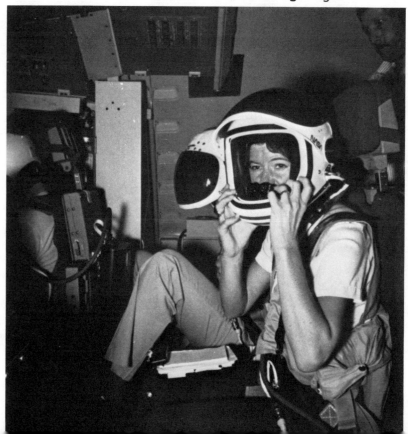

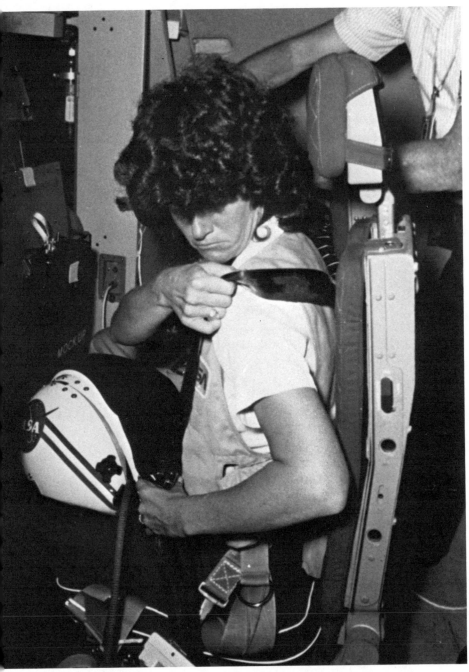

Ride adjusting herself in the Shuttle Mission Simulator.

months of rehearsals, and an agonizing wait when the Challenger's first flight had to be postponed for two months. Their own mission was thus delayed, giving them more time for practice as they went through every phase of the flight.

It had been hard not to go stale, not to let the repetition of the rehearsal keep the crew from being alert for every function they'd now be performing, but they were working for perfection. No one let down.

Everyone is trained to take over all crew members' duties. Even though the mission specialists are not trained as pilots, they have been given enough hours of instruction so that in an emergency they could land the Shuttle.

At T-3.8 seconds the computers command the three engines to fire. They are more complex than the engines that sent the Apollos to the moon. At this point the spacecraft is operated by computers. Every throttle, every valve is checked and tested 50 times a second. Any abnormality shows up on the flashing control panels in the Shuttle and at Mission Control in Houston.

The first engine starts at T-3.46 seconds, followed by the other two at 120-millisecond intervals. There is a mighty roar, and the spacecraft shudders for a few seconds, still held down on the launch pad. There is a burst of flame and a billow of steam. Two more seconds and the solid booster power ignites.

Every one of the crew has felt these same sensations in the flight simulators used to train them for this mission, but this is for real.

Liftoff comes at exactly T + 3 seconds. The launch tower drops off. As if in slow motion, the rocket gains speed, and they are shooting through the sky, a trail of white vapor tracking them. There is no time yet to enjoy the view. Sally Ride is busy keeping an eye on the blinking dials and calling out data on her checklist.

The strongest 3 "g" push comes and goes quickly two minutes into the flight, just before the solid-fuel rocket boosters have burned off their fuel and dropped by parachute into the ocean. The Shuttle is arcing upside down over the ocean. The last acceleration comes 5 minutes later and lasts a minute. The big belly tank is now empty and drops off.

Two other engines ignite at the rear of the Orbiter. They are midgets by comparison, but the Challenger is now traveling at the speed of 17,400 miles an hour. Exactly 8 minutes and 20 seconds after lift-off the Challenger is orbiting 184 miles above the Earth. 44 minutes and 23.7 seconds after its thunderous launch from Cape Canaveral, the Shuttle reaches its final orbiting position beyond the fringe of the Earth's atmosphere.

A NASA spokesman announces on the airwaves, "Space Shuttle Challenger has delivered to space the largest human payload of all time, four men and one woman." Never before had more than four people been sent aloft at one time. And Sally Ride, at age 32, had also made another record as the youngest American astronaut to fly in space.

Sally Ride standing by a model of a Space Shuttle Orbiter.

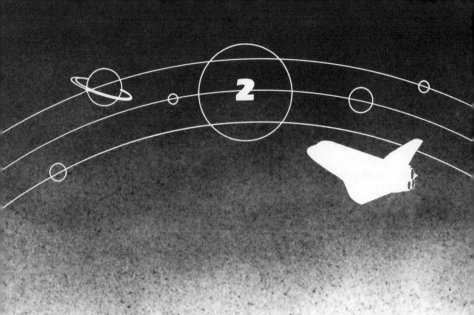

FLOATING FREE

Gradually there is a sense of weightlessness. An arm raised to reach forward has a will of its own. It tends to float upward to shoulder height. Suddenly tension eases. Grins appear on all five faces, and an unidentified whoop of enthusiasm is beamed down to Houston.

"How is it up there?" Mission Communicator Roy Bridges asks.

Sally Ride's answer comes bubbling back from outer space. "Have you ever been to Disneyland? Well, this is definitely an 'E' ticket." The "E" ticket was once the premium pass for the spectacular rides.

Commander Crippen, the only one of the astronauts who has been up in space before, reports that there is really nothing to report at the moment. Sally Ride interrupts, "I'm not so sure I'd go along with that."

All are now unbuckled from their launch harnesses. Helmets are removed. They have been advised to move slowly at first in the unaccustomed weightlessness to avoid what some space travelers had experienced before, a queasy feeling in the pit of the stomach, not so affectionately known as space-adaption syndrome. Dr. Thagard had been added to the original crew to observe such symptoms, to test their reflexes, and to keep his "patients" physically fit. Some are now testing their space legs by floating around the cabin.

Housekeeping chores come first. Some equipment necessary only during launch and landing is stowed below. The huge 60-foot-long clamshell-shaped doors of the cargo hold have to be opened immediately to dissipate the heat that builds up inside on liftoff.

Two hours into the mission the first television pictures of the cargo hold are sent down to Houston. The camera moves to give a magnificent view of the Earth below: its waters royal blue, its clouds creamy white, its continents beige, red, green, and dark brown, an occasional lake or river glinting silver as the sun strikes at just the right angle.

It's an extraordinarily beautiful picture that no one has really been able to put into words. The notion that whole continents can be seen at a glance tends to do away with political borders and strengthens the feeling of unity on Earth.

This is a great day for all those who have been working months to make this flight a reality, from scientists to the factory workers who helped build the equipment. They all share in a way the thrill of this view from outer space.

The camera next focuses on the Shuttle crew. Each one is busy at a particular chore scheduled precisely on their work sheets, but there is still time for a grin at the camera, a wave to the watching world. It is obvious the astronauts are having fun.

Appetites that had been ignored in the early morning hours now demand attention. Everyone is to have a turn at meal preparation. It has been made clear that just because a woman is aboard, she is not the only one expected to serve up the food.

There have been a lot of changes for the better in the type of menu that is offered to space travelers compared to what John Glenn sampled more than twenty years ago. One of the most important experiments assigned to Glenn was to eat a meal in zero gravity. Some worried that it would be hard to swallow in weightless space. Could food be forced into the stomach?

Glenn found that eating was easy once the food was in his mouth, but there wasn't much pleasure in the experience. Nourishment was packaged either in toothpaste-type tubes or in bite-size cubes. Crumbs from the cubes caused plenty of problems as they floated around the interior of the cabin, fouling instruments. A gummy gelatin was used as coating on later flights.

At first it was thought that any food in an open bowl would fly away. Then it was discovered that food mixed with heavy sauces and gravies would stick to the dish.

Food is now preserved in several ways. Some items are dehydrated or freeze-dried. Other foods, such as meat, are packed in foil ready to eat. They have been thermostabilized. This means they have been heated enough to kill bacteria and prevent spoilage. Breads are treated with radiation to keep them fresh. Only a few snacks, such as nuts, granola bars, and Life Savers, are eaten in their natural form.

The galley (kitchen area) of the Shuttle is a self-contained unit about the size of a food dispenser, the kind where you put your money in a slot and out comes a candy bar or soft drink.

Menus are planned for nutrition, but they are also planned to taste good and to look as attractive as possible. How can gourmet meals be served in space when everyone is busy working on out-of-this-world problems? It's just a matter of on-earth planning. Shuttle meals are assembled from pre-cooked food, and packaged in individual portions. Individual servings are assembled into meals, overwrapped, and packed in pouches. Each pouch is marked by day and meal. Some items need to be heated, others rehydrated by adding water to the pouch through a hollow needle. For liquids, a plastic straw with a clamp on it is inserted into the container.

Snacks are part of the pantry supplies. However, the preplanned balanced diet furnishes about 3,000 calories per day. Meals are chosen that have a minimum of roughage and items that are hard to digest. Seasonings, such as salt and pepper, come in liquid packages. It was discovered that most food seasoned as the astronauts would enjoy it on Earth seems very bland. This is caused by a certain nasal congestion that is experienced in zero gravity. Smell is so related to taste that spicier condiments are added.

Silverware, a can opener, and a pair of scissors to open the packets are standard equipment. They are held in place with magnets on the tray. The tray is fastened to a table the same way.

It was planned to have four astronauts eat at a time. One would always stay on the flight deck to monitor the workings of the Shuttle.

The first meal for the astronauts is the hardest to adjust to. Everyone is standing, holding him- or herself in place with the help of suction cups on the heel and ball of their soft slippers. Doubling up in a sitting position in space requires muscles. Some try it, but soon give up.

There is plenty of kidding at their clumsiness, but good manners are a must in zero gravity. Stick a spoon or fork into a sticky dish, and it is coated on all sides—nothing drops off. Scrape it on the side of the dish, but be sure that the excess stays in place. If not, it is apt to float toward the ceiling or even land on a neighbor's head. One such mishap occurs on this flight, but it is caught butterfly-net-style with a whoop of laughter.

For dessert someone suggests they open the jar of jellybeans provided by President Reagan. There is a contest to see who can catch them fastest in midair, no hands allowed.

There's a relaxed attitude on Flight 7. Of course, there's plenty of terse, businesslike space jargon bandied back and forth among the astronauts as they go about their business, but there are moments of humor and kidding that help break the tension.

At one point Ride reports that there are "three turkeys and two hams" aboard, although she didn't identify them. This brings on hoots of laughter.

Is it because a woman is aboard, or did Crippen break the mold of the always-serious, stern commander? It is clear to those eavesdropping that everyone is having a ball.

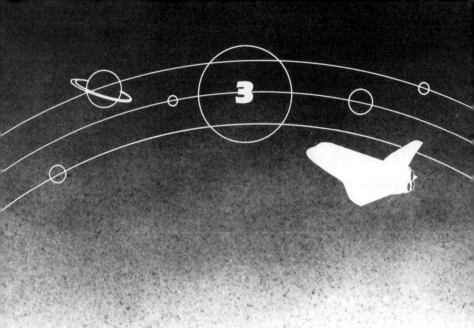

SATELLITE AWAY

Some of the crew have washed up before the meal. It's pretty hard to get dirty in this environment. Some may want to use the bathroom. There's always plenty of water aboard the Shuttle because it manufactures its own in outer space. The Shuttle's electricity is produced by three fuel cells. Each has 32 plates. When liquid hydrogen is applied to one side of the plate and liquid oxygen to the other, electrical power is generated. The byproduct is pure, crystal clear water.

No showers have been provided for short missions. Sponge baths are the order of the day. A personal hygiene station is on the side of the galley. It has a light, a mirror, and a hand washing enclosure. Astronauts place their hands through flexible cuffs in a spray chamber. Water is forced in a jet stream into the chamber, then immediately sucked back into the disposal tank so that droplets won't be floating around the cabin.

Every astronaut has his or her personal hygiene kit. This includes chemically coated washcloths and towels, and small items, such as a toothbrush, toothpaste, dental floss, nail clippers, soap, stick deodorant, a comb, a brush, and antichap lipstick and also skin lotion because of the dryness of air aboard the Shuttle. For male crew members the kit also contains a tube of shaving cream and a safety razor or a wind-up shaver.

Female astronauts will be provided with tampons if their menstrual period occurs during the flight. Even this equipment has been designed for space. Someone made the suggestion that the tampons be strung together like link sausages, so that they wouldn't float around the cabin if one slipped out of its case. Now they come in a chain and can be snipped free when needed.

The bathroom on the Shuttle has been made to look as much like home as possible. There's a light over the right shoulder to read by, and the hatch window on the left gives the user an out–of–this–

world view. But there are some drastic differences in the plumbing.

To use the toilet, or WCS (waste collection system), as it's called in space talk, an astronaut first opens the door and extends a pair of privacy curtains. To remain seated an astronaut must insert his or her soft shoe into the toeholds of foot restraints and snap together a seat belt.

To the right of the commode is a handle and control panel. When the handle is in the forward position the toilet gate valve opens. Air is drawn through the toilet by a fan so that any waste material is carried downward, as it would be with gravity, to a compartment below. A set of vanes, called the slinger, in this compartment begins to shred solid waste and deposit it in a thin layer on the chemically treated walls of the waste compartment. When the handle is in an off position, the gate closes and the vent valve opens so that the chamber is in the vacuum of space. This very quickly dries the waste, and it can be sucked into a holding receptacle. Liquid waste moves in an airflow system into a separate tank and is periodically dumped overboard.

There is still one very important job to be done before the astronauts have their first night of sleep in space. The Challenger carries two communication satellites, almost identical to the two carried on Columbia's fifth mission in November 1982. On the last trip of the Challenger there had been a malfunction of one of the satellites. It is important to have this maneuver perform exactly as planned to prove to the world that this is a very practical use for this expensive spacecraft. NASA is being paid $11 million to deliver them in space.

On the Challenger's seventh orbit, mission specialists Fabian and Ride start the countdown. Every one of the crew watches tensely through the rear window of the flight deck that views the cargo area. First they set Canada's Anik satellite spinning on its turntable at 50 revolutions per minute so that it won't wobble out of orbit when ejected. About 20 minutes later computers command the clamps to blow. A spring gives the final push, sending the five-ton cylindrical satellite on its six-day climb to a much higher orbit. A slight nudge is all that is felt inside the cabin.

Under its own power, the satellite is scheduled to reach a height of 22,300 miles above the Earth's surface. It will orbit there at precisely the correct speed to remain stationary over a prearranged point on Earth. Scientists call it a geostationary orbit.

The crew congratulates themselves on a job well done so far, but there are 21 other experiments aboard the Shuttle to attend to and one more satellite to launch. Tomorrow will be busy.

Night comes every 90 minutes on their flight, so sleep must be scheduled by the clock, not the sun. Four bunks are provided for the crew. A fifth member is always alert on the flight deck. Across the mid-deck from the galley is a small alcove with what appears to be a double-decker bunk. Actually it can provide sleeping room for four persons, because with zero gravity there's no up or down, top or bottom.

The first person floats into the top bunk, the second the lower bunk. The third sleeper's bed is on the backside of the lower bunk and faces the floor. The fourth astronaut is sleeping on his feet, so to speak, as his bunk is set vertically against one end of the two-level bunk.

Each bed is a padded board with a fireproof sleeping bag attached with just enough pressure to create the illusion of a comfortable mattress. The astronauts' arms are slipped under straps to keep them in place. On earlier missions astronauts slept in tethered sleeping bags without any back support. Their sleep was restless.

Each sleeping space is slightly more than 6 feet in length, 30 inches wide. There's a small light and an airflow duct by each bunk. Eyeshades and earmuffs are available to cut out light and noise, but it's a strange sensation, and sleep does not come right away.

Sally Ride tucks herself in, draws a privacy curtain across her small space, and tries not to feel the hum of the pulsing spacecraft.

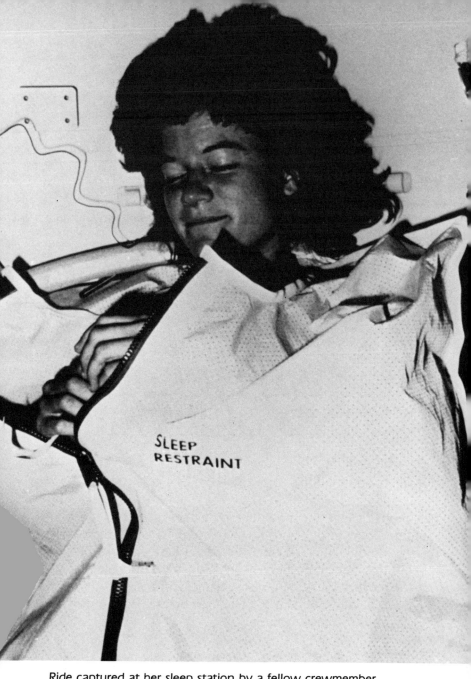

SLEEP
RESTRAINT

Ride captured at her sleep station by a fellow crewmember
while in flight. She is using the sleep restraint device.

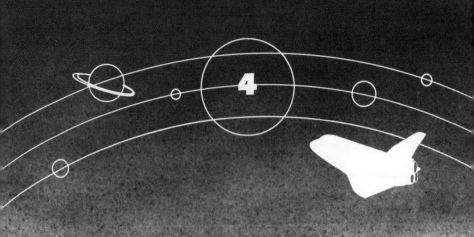

"WE PICK UP AND DELIVER"

The next morning NASA wakes the crew with a "Rise and Shine" program of lively music, although most of them admit to being awake before the cheery send-off. Sally Ride is the only one not to receive Father's Day greetings from the ground for the "dads on board." The men on the flight have ten children among them.

Each person has a specific routine to follow, but the most important item on the day's agenda is the launching of the second satellite, Palapa B. When aloft it will provide a much needed boost in television and telephone communication to the more than 13,000 scattered islands of Indonesia.

Once more the signal is given. Again the drum-shaped satellite swirls out of its launch platform right on schedule.

The next picture of the astronauts shows four of them wearing identical blue tee shirts with white lettering that reads, "TFNG. WE DELIVER." They are lined up arm-to-arm grinning like impish kids. It is explained that TFNG stands for "Thirty-five New Guys," the number recruited for the astronaut class of 1978. Only Crippen, an "old guy" from the class of '69, was not allowed to wear one.

A voice from Houston assures him, "That's all right, Crip. We can tell you're a steely-eyed veteran from here."

There is little relaxing between chores. Dr. Norm Thagard seems to have the easiest job because the crew is in such top condition. He continues to monitor heartbeat and respiration when the astronauts are at rest and when they perform on a treadmill.

Sally Ride comments, "I'm probably one of the few people ever to run across the Indian Ocean."

There are experiments to activate in the cabin area and by remote control in the payload bay. One of the seven Getaway Specials, those small canis-

Ride stands in the mid-deck of the **Challenger** near one of the experiments to which she has devoted a great deal of time.

ters in the cargo hold, is sold by NASA for $3,000 to $10,000. One contains a colony of ants to be observed on TV. How are they affected by zero gravity? Another contains radish seeds to see how plants can tell where to "lay down" their roots. Another experiment concerns the formation of crystals in microgravity.

The mission specialists are in charge of what might be called our first space factory. In a process known as electrophoresis, electrical fields separate biological compounds of protein with greater purity than can be accomplished on Earth. A representative from the firm of McDonnell Douglas has reported that, "Our long-range goal is to install a production unit in some kind of Earth-orbiting facility by 1989." The STS-7 crew is helping to set up the prototype model.

Plenty of serious work was being done, but the crew never once lost their sense of humor. On the end of the third day the five astronauts and Mission Control did a comic routine copied from an old television series, "The Waltons," passing out "good-nights" to one another, name by name, including "Good night, John Boy."

It wound up with astronaut John Fabian sending a good night wish to his wife Donna in a disguised voice using Jimmy Durante's classic line, "Goodnight, Mrs. Calabash, wherever you are."

The broadcast ended with Sally Ride asking, "Who was that masked man?" straight out of the Lone Ranger. These exchanges were followed by the recorded sound of crickets chirping.

The mission's highlight comes on the fifth day. The robot arm in the payload bay is to be used for the first time. One of the reasons Sally Ride was chosen for this mission was her experience with the remote manipulator system, the RMS. This is a 50-foot-long boom, roughly the diameter of a telephone pole. It is jointed in four places and has a grapple and a television camera at its free end. It can be bent, folded, swiveled, swung, and extended by remote control from the cabin compartment of the Shuttle.

Ride and pilot Hauck go over procedures in operating the remote manipulator system in the Johnson Space Center's Shuttle engineering simulator.

The job of the mission specialists is to pick up a 3,300-pound self-contained lab, the West German-built Shuttle Pallet Satellite, or SPAS, very carefully and set it adrift outside the Challenger. Aboard the $23 million package is a remote controlled television camera and eight experiments. In space those experiments can be conducted with less vibration than aboard the Shuttle. This SPAS is to monitor the effect of the Shuttle on its immediate environment. It is also to be used as a very convenient item to be retrieved from space, a job

Ride at the Kennedy Space Center to participate in a Mission Sequence Test with the Shuttle Pallet Satellite.

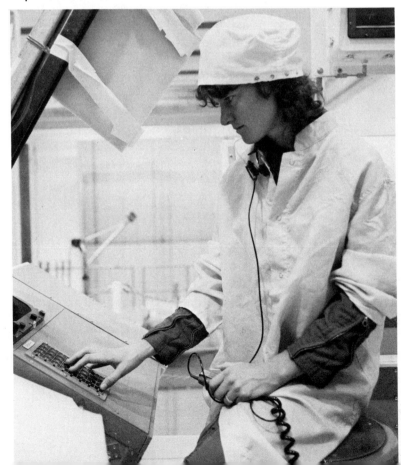

that will be even more important in the future in repairing malfunctioning satellites.

Again Sally Ride and John Fabian stand before the computer console on the aft flight deck. Ride calls out commands. Fabian punches buttons that activate the huge arm. Carefully and in slow motion, a snarelike device at the end of the arm grabs hold of the satellite and lifts it out of the spaceship. Now it floats free, following the same speed as the spaceship. Almost immediately, the astronauts snatch it back.

Finding there are no problems with the RMS, they let the flying lab float free again, and the Challenger moves away, using its small thruster maneuvering engines. Five times Ride and Fabian retrieve and release the satellite, taking turns at the controls. Dr. Thagard is allowed to work the manipulator on one catch. He has been training as their backup, if needed.

For the first time spectacular pictures of the orbiting Challenger are shown on the screen, taken from a distance of a thousand feet by the flying lab SPAS.

"Beautiful," exclaims Guy Gardner from Mission Control in Houston.

"You've got five very happy people up here," Astronaut Rick Hauck says.

"There are several thousand happy people down here," Gardner replies.

The SPAS is finally tucked away in the cargo hold to be used on another mission.

When all is secured, Crippen announces proudly, "We've been told some crews in the past

Ride familiarizes herself with activity involving the Space Shuttle's remote manipulator system.

have claimed, 'We deliver.' Well, for Flight Seven, 'We pick up and deliver.'"

So far everything has been on schedule, just as the crew had practiced the mission. In space talk, there were far fewer anomalies than on any previous flight—an anomaly being a "glitch," a "screw-up," or an unexpected malfunction of some system.

It isn't until the fifth day in orbit that the crew learned the big glitch is something they can't control. Storm clouds are hugging the Florida coast.

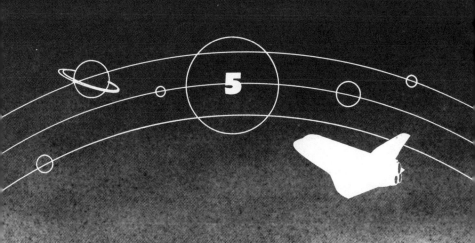

WEATHER GLITCH

STS-7 was scheduled to be the first Shuttle flight to land on the runway adjacent to Cape Canaveral. A new three-mile landing strip had been prepared. This was where pilots Crippen and Hauck had been practicing touchdowns.

Nothing is ever planned on a space mission without a contingency procedure. If a Florida landing definitely had to be cancelled, it would be back to the dry lake bed in the California Mojave Desert. All other Shuttle flights had used this huge, natural, flat piece of land that allowed for plenty of lee-way in set-down space. If the original plans were to be scrapped, it would be a disappointment.

The Florida landing site would save considerable money and time in readying the Challenger for its next mission. Otherwise, the Shuttle would have to be flown piggyback to the Cape for the next launch. Precious days would be lost in a tight schedule, and the flight would drain money from an already tight budget.

Besides, the press, visiting dignitaries, even the President of the United States, were all planning to greet the arrival of the Challenger on the East coast. It is a difficult decision to make. Consultations flash back and forth through the airwaves.

At first it is thought feasible to delay the date of the landing to see if the Florida weather will clear. The astronauts cheerfully agree with this decision. They say they will gladly stay aloft for a few more swings around their home planet.

Then the gauges monitoring one of the auxiliary power units that control the steering and braking systems during landing begin developing quirks. There'd be no problem if the backup units hold, but on this special flight that affects the entire NASA program, no one wants to take any unnecessary risks. Besides, much to the glee of native Californians, their weather is more predictable than what can be expected at the Cape.

Finally Lt. Gen. James Abrahamson, head of the Shuttle program, sends word to the crew that on their next-to-the-last orbit they are to reprogram their reentry time and start their long glide home to the desert runway at Edwards Air Force Base.

Crippen acknowledges the change of plans with more than a trace of disappointment. "Well, we would like to have gone there (Florida) very much, but if the weather's bad, that's not the right thing to do."

The crew slip into specially designed leggings or antigravity pants. The pants are laced with tubing that can be inflated to put pressure on the lower part of the body. On reentry there is a sudden flow of the body fluids to legs and feet, reducing blood supply in the head. If this happens too suddenly, it can cause blackouts. The astronauts have all been tested for stronger "G's" than are expected now with no ill effects, but the leggings are a safeguard.

The crew once again strap themselves into the contoured seats they used during takeoff. They will feel the pressure of gravity as their ship slams into the Earth's atmosphere.

The descent starts when the Shuttle is orbiting 200 miles (320 kilometers) above the ground at a speed of over 17,000 miles per hour (27,000 kph) and ends on a runway half a world away with no more fuel left in its tanks to change course in case of an emergency.

Figures have been run through computers. The pilot and crew have gone through the procedure, not dozens, but hundreds of times in flight simulators, but still there is an anxious feeling when the first burn is made, knowing how precisely every procedure must be carried out.

To prepare the deorbit burn, the pilot first turns the Shuttle around so that it is traveling tail first. This permits the rear thruster engines of the orbital maneuvering system (OMS) engines to put on the brakes, so to speak, by giving the Shuttle a short blast of pressure in the opposite direction it is drifting. These small thrusters are fired for two or three minutes. The exact firing time depends on the weight of the Shuttle and its payload. The speed is reduced about 200 miles per hour.

Now the Shuttle is turned around again so that it is flying nose first and nose up, presenting the heavier insulated belly of the craft to the increasingly denser layers of air. About half an hour after the first deorbit burn, the Shuttle has descended to an altitude of 400,000 feet. The space vehicle hits molecules of air so fast and so hard that the air cannot effectively get out of the way. There is a transfer of energy to heat, heat that soars to 2,700 degrees Fahrenheit. The porous insulating tiles are the lifesaving protection against this fiery inferno.

The hot air turns to a blazing, electrified gas that envelops the outer shell of the spacecraft and blocks transmission of radio signals. This blackout trajectory lasts several minutes. Everyone at Mission Control waits anxiously. The crew is busy watching numbers flash across their computer screens.

Another plane has been in the air since dawn on a special assignment to take one picture of the Challenger's descent. It's not just an ordinary snapshot they're hoping for, but an infrared picture showing the heating of Challenger's underbelly. Are there certain hot spots that need improved protection?

This plane is not an agile fighter that can quickly maneuver. Instead, NASA converted a C-141 transport into an airborne observatory. Behind the cockpit a research quality telescope is mounted. They hadn't expected to be called into action for the STS-7 landing, but they are ready.

Suddenly, there's a shout in the observatory plane. "The tracker has it." The massive telescope swings into action. Seconds later a hot blur flashes into view and is gone. The Shuttle was moving at nearly 16 times the speed of sound and dropping at almost two miles per second. The observatory plane came no closer than 32 miles from the streaking Shuttle, but in less than 1/125 of a second its job is completed.

At a lower altitude two fast chase planes will angle closer for action pictures of the approach and landing.

At 78,000 feet Crippen switches from automatic pilot and takes over control for the wide sweeping turn to line up his glider with the black painted stripe on a dazzling white patch of packed earth below him. The craft drops out of the sky. It has no power. Its fuel has been used up in its tremendous vault into space. Entering the Earth's atmosphere, its stubby wings must catch the heavier air at just the right angle to buoy it for a perfect on-target landing. There are no second chances. A pilot can't swoop up and make another pass if calculations are wrong.

The early morning sun catches the arrow shape of the Shuttle high in the sky. Only a small number of people are on hand to see the Challenger come in, but they carry some hurriedly made signs, one proclaiming, "HERSTORY MADE TODAY BY SALLY RIDE."

One last graceful bank over the stark California landscape, and the landing gear is locked into place. The Shuttle now looks almost like a normal passenger ship approaching the airfield. It is hard to believe that in its 98-orbit flight the Shuttle has traveled 2.5 million miles.

It is a perfect landing. Again there are whoops of joy from inside the cabin, whoops sounding vaguely similar to those on the day of the launch.

Crippen radios, "As I said once before, this is a perfect way to come to California."

Back at the Cape, thousands watch on television the sight they had planned to see live. The capcom from Mission Control sends his message, "Congratulations! The good news is that the beer is very, very cold this morning. The bad news is that it is 3,000 miles away."

Sally Ride's mother and father are disappointed not to see their daughter immediately. "We live only a hundred miles from the California runway.

We could have stayed at home." Joyce Ride laughs, for she has no real complaints.

President Reagan speaks to the crew on the telephone, congratulating them all, but particularly singling out Sally Ride. He assures her that she was chosen for the mission because, "You were the best person for the job." Sally Ride is not a token woman for the world to praise.

Ride's own way of summing up the past 146 hours was, "The thing that I'll remember most about the flight is that it was fun," she said. "In fact, I'm sure it was the most fun I will ever have in my life."

No one is going to agree wholeheartedly with that statement, knowing Sally has had fun in many ways all her life. NASA was even then planning on sending her on another space flight.

Sally Ride.

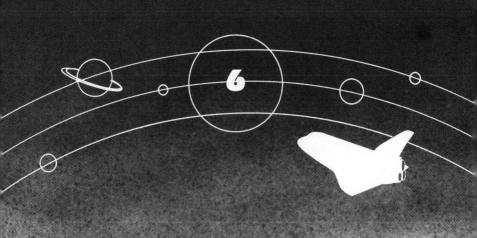

SALLY RIDE

Sally Ride doesn't consider herself the extra-ordinary person she is. She has a knack for turning off the glare of the spotlight as if pulling down a shade.

A *Washington Post* reporter asked how she deals with the nuisance of being a celebrity. She explained that she solves the problem by flipping the switch "oblivious."

She rarely offers information about herself unless asked, and she's been asked some pretty dumb questions lately. One reporter queried, "Do you weep when you have a problem?"

She kept her cool by answering, "Why don't you ask Rick that question?" Rick is crew member Navy Commander Frederick H. Hauck.

Was she going to wear a bra in outer space? "There's no sag in zero G."

Yes, she enjoyed reading science fiction when she was young, but she also liked Nancy Drew.

No, she is not a health food nut. She sometimes goes on binges of hamburgers and fries.

On TV Jane Pauley asked whether Dr. Ride thought she'd be watched more closely than the other astronauts because she was a woman. Ride turned the question back to the reporter. "It seems to me I ought to be asking you that question."

Her family has been in the spotlight too. Her dad teaches political science at Santa Monica Community College and has the title of assistant to the superintendent of the college. Her mother, Joyce, stayed at home with Sally and her kid sister, Karen, known by her childhood nickname of Bear, when they were growing up. Now her mother teaches English to foreign students and does volunteer work in a women's prison. Bear, two years younger than Sally, is a Presbyterian minister.

Mrs. Ride laughs when asked what she and her husband did right to produce such brilliant achievers. "In a way, you could look at it as neglect. Dale and I simply forgot to tell them there were things they couldn't do. But," she adds, "I think if it had occurred to us to tell them, we would have refrained." She taught her daughters to excel, not to conform.

On second thought, there were two activities in Sally's life her mom admits she might have influenced, one in a negative way. She forced Sally to take piano lessons. Sally had no interest at the time in music and promptly turned practice sessions into a grind. Her mother's more positive suggestion was that instead of setting her goal to be a member of the Los Angeles Dodgers baseball team, she might like to play tennis.

Sally has always liked sports, even as a freckle-faced little girl who often talked her way into a game of football or baseball with boys if she couldn't round up a game of her own. Her dad remembers that she used to read the sports pages rather than the comics as a kid.

She started playing tennis when she was ten. She was good, and with serious practice she got better. At eleven she was taking lessons from four-time women's champion Alice Marble. She entered tournaments and won, being nationally ranked in her early teens.

Billie Jean King watched her play and suggested she leave school and turn professional. It was a tough decision to make with praise from such a high source, but there were too many other things Sally wanted to learn off the courts.

She's been quoted as saying she decided against life as a pro because her backhand wasn't strong enough. Her sister Bear says that Sally lacks the "killer instinct" for professional sports. A good friend suggests that it was just boredom that set in. There were other goals to attain.

Boredom was the only stumbling block Sally ever had to conquer in school. She had always been a good student, but if a subject didn't interest her, she'd turn to daydreaming. One teacher saw her as a clock watcher. Sally remembers the teacher was dull and the class wasn't interesting enough to keep her from doodling and squirming.

When there was something fun to learn, you couldn't keep her nose out of a book. The year before she started playing tennis her father took a year's leave of absence from his teaching job, and the family traveled through Europe. Sally remembers it was a surprise to her that people all looked the same, even when they spoke different languages. The hotels were different, and the food wasn't the same, and every day there was a new routine and new sights. It was a wonderful year. When Sally reentered school, she was moved half a grade ahead of her group.

Sally agrees that her parents often let her select what she wanted to do, but then she adds with a smile, "Once the decision was made, you know, we had to do it. My father made sure I studied and I brought home the right kind of grades."

Science was her love in high school. She credits one very remarkable teacher she had at Westlake High School. Elizabeth Mommaerts taught physiology. Sally remembers it wasn't particularly the subject as much as the scientific method of her approach to the class that stirred interest. "I had never seen logic personified before," said Sally.

In high school she took courses in physiology, chemistry, physics, trigonometry, and calculus, so that when the time came for college science, she was well prepared.

She remained a close friend of Elizabeth Mommaerts until her teacher's death in 1972.

"She was the one person in the world I most wanted to call (after being selected astronaut), even more than my parents," Sally says.

Dr. Ride went to Swarthmore College for one year but transferred to Stanford University as a sophomore, principally because she wanted to continue playing serious tournament tennis.

She played number one on the Stanford tennis team and was a star rugby player as well. She graduated with distinction from Stanford with a B.S. in physics and a B.A. in English. "Like most science majors, I'd been taking all science majors, and I needed some sanity courses," Sally explains. "So I signed up for a course in Shakespeare. I liked it and just kept on taking that sort of thing."

She never got less than an A in English either. Her roommate, Molly Tyson, now a technical writer for Apple Computer, remembers, "She wrote English papers the way she wrote science papers. She would turn in three pages and that was it. But she would always see to the heart of things. Her style was to quickly think, figure it out, crystallize it. What she said was very convincing, so there was no need to continue."

Sally's also a very resourceful person, Tyson remembers. Sally's car once broke down on a lonely road when the two of them were returning from a vacation weekend. Tyson was sure they'd have to wait until someone came to their rescue. Sally knew enough about what was under the hood of her Toyota to realize that a bit of Scotch tape could repair a leaking radiator hose. After digging around in the trunk of the car she found a saucepan once used on a camping trip and headed down the road to find a water supply.

Tyson laughs when she says it's one of the few times she'd ever seen Sally pick up a kitchen pan. "I only lied once," Tyson says, "when questioned by the FBI about Sally's personality traits when they were considering her astronaut application. But I figured that dust and dirty dishes wouldn't accumulate in a space capsule the way they had in our apartment."

It is a trait Sally probably inherited from her nondomestic mother, who puts priorities on intellectual pursuits, not housework.

Molly describes the Ride family as a loving, easygoing family. No one was required to sit at the same table for dinner. People ate what they liked, and if it was cheese and crackers and nuts, that was all right too. Perhaps it is the lack of gourmet home cooking that has Ride stating that the dehydrated, thermostabilized space provisions are pretty good, her roommate adds.

With a degree in both science and English, she had to make a choice if she were to continue graduate work. She turned to her first love, science. She had made the right choice at the right time. She chose astronomy as her major and narrowed her interest to X-ray astronomy and free electron lasers. Her study was in the theoretical behavior of free electrons in a magnetic field, an investigation carried out almost in the abstract as sets of equations. Some day this background could lead to the study of ways to transmit power from orbiting space stations to Earth, but she has never set out for herself a narrow goal to follow.

Fred Hargadon, dean of admissions at UCLA, says, "She always left a little room in her life for things to happen." Flexibility has been an asset.

Sally Ride heard about the call for scientist astronauts by reading an article in a campus newspaper. She was winding up her doctorate at Stanford and looking for a postdoctoral spot in laser physics.

"I don't know why I wanted to do it. I honestly can't tell you what was going through my mind. I only know I was on my way out of the room to apply while I was still reading the notice in the paper."

When the call was issued in 1978, NASA was swamped. 8,079 people applied. 1,544 were women. Everyone's record was carefully reviewed. 208 finalists in groups of 20 were summoned to the Johnson Space Center near Houston for interviews.

"Nobody knew what to expect. From what we'd heard and read, we thought they'd put us in centrifuges, dunk us in ice water, hang us by the toes, anything."

Instead, the applicants were met by a team of doctors who put them through a strenuous stress test on a treadmill.

"We look for good, overall conditioning, not

superhuman strength or endurance," says Dr. Berry, who helped conduct the testing. "We take into account each candidate's weight in relationship to his or her body build. We weren't half as tough on the applicants as they were on themselves. Basically we were observing how their hearts function under conditions of maximum exercise to pick up blood pressure problems or an irregular heartbeat. But no matter what we told them, the applicants figure this must be *the* fitness test. And although this was not an endurance test, they were secretly competing to see who could stay on the treadmill the longest."

This was no problem for Sally, who keeps in shape with top-flight tennis and jogging five miles a day. A thorough check of her medical history from day one showed she was in top condition.

Each candidate was interviewed by two psychiatrists. "The first guy was what I would have expected," Sally says. "You sat in a big, easy chair and made yourself comfortable. He was very warm. 'Tell me about yourself. Do you love your mother? Why do you love her? How does your sister feel about you?' Freudian things, I guess, but I'm not into psychology."

The second psychiatrist played the role of Mister Bad Guy. He snapped orders like, "Five-seven-four-one-three. Repeat that backwards." She did, and he gave her another set of figures, again and again, until she failed. The questions kept coming with no chance of getting them all right. Sally began to sense what the psychiatrist was trying to do—put her on edge—but she managed to keep her cool.

Finally, there was an hour-long interview with the ten-member selection committee. Dr. Carolyn Huntoon was the only woman on the board. Sally remembers it was like orals for her Ph.D.," but with one exception. There was absolutely nothing you could do to prepare for it."

The committee asked her about her hobbies and her childhood. "I don't know why, because they had it all on paper in front of them, but I just told them what they wanted to know. They were very pleasant and courteous, and they said, 'Thank you.' That's all."

It was a long wait to hear the next news. Sally admits she was sure some women would be chosen, but would she be one of them?

"Women in space were inevitable," she says. "At the very least they need us up there for biological experiments. Also, we're part of a change in attitude toward astronauts. We're not godlike infallible people, but technicians, scientists who will make outer space accessible to the average person and help build space colonies of the future. That's an incredible thing to be part of."

About a month after the interviews Sally got a call from George Abbey, who is in charge of flight operation, asking if she was still interested. The answer was a resounding, "Absolutely."

She immediately called her family. Her mother was just as excited as Sally, but she hadn't lost her sense of humor. "I knew at least one of you girls was going to get to Heaven."

"I think I'll even beat my minister sister," Sally said with a grin. She has.

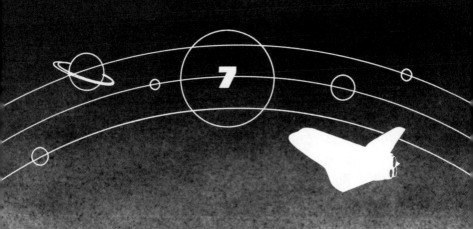

JUDITH RESNIK

Judith Resnik—second American woman in space. Judy will be aboard the maiden voyage of the third Shuttle, Discovery.

There may be stars in Judy's eyes, but her feet are planted firmly on the ground. She is a very practical person. She doesn't sit around and wait for things to happen to her. She lays out a plan of strategy to make sure that they do. She hasn't let excitement cloud her vision of what is likely to happen to her own life plans and job future. She's measured the advantages and disadvantages carefully.

Judy was brought up in Akron, Ohio. Her father was an optometrist, her mother a legal secretary. She started school at age four, and early on proved to be a very bright youngster. Her powers of concentration were unusual for a child of her age.

Other kids on the block were taking music lessons, but none applied themselves with Judy's diligence to become a child prodigy at the piano. Judy not only showed talent, but a willingness to spend hours at practice. She has continued her musical interest, and at one time considered a career as a concert pianist.

But as with every one of the woman astronauts, she didn't limit herself to just one interest. Science was her major field, even in high school. Judy worked her way through Carnegie Mellon University, graduating in 1970 as an electrical engineer.

"I must have been asked a thousand times why a woman would want to be an electrical engineer. All I can say is it appealed to me. If I want something, I want it."

With that determination, she went on to earn her doctorate from the University of Maryland. Her professional honors are impressive. She started designing integrated circuitry for radio control systems for RCA and then worked for the NASA sounding rocket program and telemetry systems, all very important projects in space research.

She also veered into another field of research as

a biomedical engineer at the National Institute of Health in Bethesda, Maryland, from 1974 to 1977, where she studied the inner workings of the eye, a subject she'd heard a lot about from her father.

Immediately preceding her selection as an astronaut candidate, she was a senior systems engineer in product development with the Xerox Corporation in California. Judy is not only a very bright person, but she has determination and a highly developed sense of curiosity. For her, there's always another field of interest to explore.

"Becoming an astronaut wasn't a lifelong dream for me, as it was for some people," she admits candidly. But she felt a job with NASA would further her career, so she went after that job.

From the time Judy heard on a Washington, DC talk show that NASA was looking for its first female candidates in space, she wanted the job. She figured out mathematically just what she thought her chances were, to avoid any horrible disappointment. She came up with four in twenty. Then she set out to improve those odds.

To condition herself physically, she started a regular routine of running. Then to make herself more familiar with the aims and history of NASA, she paid frequent visits to the National Air and Space Museum in Washington. She met its director, Apollo astronaut Michael Collins, and explained the reason for her intense interest. She was planning on becoming an astronaut herself. Collins wished her well, but he'd heard that speech before.

"I talked to my congressman too," she says,

"but for all I knew NASA was planning on picking names out of a hat."

She also started taking flying lessons, not that she thought she'd be able to match experience with commercial or military pilots, but it might give her a slight edge over the competition.

Judy was living alone in a Redondo Beach, California singles complex when she applied. Her attitude about life is refreshingly straightforward.

"I do what I want to do. I'm single, so I don't have to explain myself to anyone. I'm pretty calm," she says, "sort of competitive too."

She prides herself on that independence. "I don't have a lot of friends that I like to call close," she admits. "I value my privacy and keeping my thoughts to myself."

Yet Judy does not live the life of a recluse. She's a gourmet chef and enjoys entertaining in small groups.

The day the news came that she had been selected an astronaut candidate, she almost missed it. She was on her way to work, and the door had closed behind her. She thought twice about returning to answer the phone. But she was glad she did.

She answered the all-important question, "Do you still want the job at NASA?" with a calm affirmative.

When later asked by the press what her first reaction was, her tongue-in-cheek reply was, "You could say I was mildly elated." But her very broad grin erases the nonemotional tinge to her words. She added that she'd very much like to go up in space right away.

Did she think she was selected to fill a role model? "No, we might be filling that role inadvertently, but that's not why we were selected. . . . We were first in our fields. We've been 'the only girls on the block,' and you get used to that early," she says.

Will it change that nicely planned, very private life of hers? Of course, but she feels it's worth it. "I'll keep up with my flying lessons and my scientific studies, no matter what happens."

What does she think her role in space, specifically as a woman, will be? "We're all astronauts," she answers, annoyed by the amount of attention being given to the women mission specialists. "We'll be going through the same training. We'll have the same problems thrown at us, and we'll have to solve them in the same ways. There are no benefits or hardships in being a woman. We're equal in this program."

She adds, "I don't see myself as having a personal mission. I'm going up there because it's something I enjoy doing, and NASA has some objectives in mind that I can help carry out in a small way. It's my opportunity to do that, and it's a challenge. . . . Progress in science is as exciting to me as sitting in a rocket is to some people. I feel less like Columbus and more like Galileo."

Judy has developed such a strict work discipline for herself over the years that she explains, "This is the first semester since I was four that I haven't been in school. I've always worked, so that I never really had a vacation. I've never traveled. I could have gone into space without even having seen California if I hadn't come here for a job."

It's a bit ironic that in one week of her life she will be traveling better than two million miles. She's certainly making up for her early stay-at-home ways.

When asked if she isn't just a little scared, she shakes her dark curly head of hair. "No, I'm more curious than apprehensive when it comes to physical challenge."

Now that she's going to be a space traveler, is she going on any specific training program apart from her running? "No, brute strength and muscle are not a premium in a weightless environment—quickness, calmness, and intelligence are. That's what we'll work with. I can't wait."

Then she adds very solemnly, "The next twelve years of my life will be great, just great."

Judy Resnik's planned it that way.

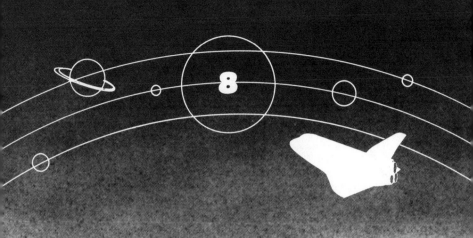

MARGARET RHEA SEDDON

Dr. Margaret Rhea Seddon (she is called Rhea, which is pronounced Ray) is a competent, highly trained surgeon. This is what is important about her selection as an astronaut. Along with her good looks, Dr. Seddon is described as having a glowing personality and an excellent sense of humor. What more could one add to all this? Intelligence and a strong sense of dedication and responsibility.

Rhea is a native of Murfreesboro, Tennessee. Her high school classmates and teachers remember that she had a burning passion to accomplish almost impossible goals. She was a leader, first in line to volunteer for jobs, enthusiastic, and always very efficient.

Rhea's father is a lawyer, her late mother was a housewife. Rhea explains, "Mother gave me a love of books and the quiet inward things, and Dad was always encouraging me to try new activities. Once when I was kind of depressed at the University of California, I complained to my father."

Rhea was thinking about going into medicine. Did she really have the stamina, the background to be successful in the field, she wondered? Nothing short of being superior would satisfy her.

She remembers his words, "You can go anyplace in the world if you really want to."

It is Rhea who has added the out-of-this-world dimension.

Dr. Seddon graduated from the University of California in Berkeley in 1970 with a B.S. in Physiology. She was accepted at the University of Tennessee College of Medicine in Memphis. It would be close to where she intended to practice her profession.

She feels strong family ties, not only to this generation, but to her family roots, her heritage. She is a member of the National Society of the Daughters of the American Revolution.

While a medical student, she took up flying. She is a member of the 99's, the International Women

Pilots Association. Every minute she could snatch from an extremely busy schedule she was up in the air. Did she think then that she might be flying even higher as an astronaut?

It seemed very improbable, yet she has always been fascinated with the exploration of space. Her face lights up with enthusiasm when she talks of colonizing space, not in the context of science fiction, but in the reality of tomorrow.

"I'd always thought being an astronaut would be a neat thing to do," she once stated, but she didn't count on it.

"I didn't know if the space program would ever be open to women," she says. "I decided to become a doctor so that if I never did get a chance, I would be able to lead a meaningful life."

That meaningful part of her life often stretched into an eighty-hour week, as she put in regular rounds at the hospital morning and evening, hours in surgery and the clinic, and working every third to fifth day on a twenty-four-hour shift. Her special interest is in the nutritional problems of postoperative patients, surgical nutrition, "feeding people by vein," she explains.

This is a relatively new field of medicine. Rhea likes to be in on the beginning of new research. She admits that "this specialization made me interesting to the space program. Also, anyone who has an M.D. has a wide scientific background."

When she applied at NASA to become an astronaut, everyone was surprised. Her sister said, "You're crazy. You're willing to pass up $100,000 a year as a surgeon to go into a $22,000-a-year job?"

That salary figure has increased slightly, but Rhea was well aware she probably had more to lose financially than any of the other women because of her earning potential. "But this is what I want to do, so I'm going to do it."

Her flying instructor had no idea she had any ambitions to become an astronaut. "It came as a complete surprise when she asked me to be one of her references."

He remembers her as "a good student, very intelligent, very determined. She did extremely well on the written tests too, of course, but I'd never really pictured her as being a daredevil type."

Rhea doesn't think of herself like that either. Being an astronaut was a chance to apply science in an exciting view of the future.

When Dr. Seddon was chosen to come to Houston, she was single and living in an apartment crammed with houseplants. She loves to cook lavish desserts. Does she have a problem with weight? She laughs, "That's a matter between my doctor at NASA and myself." Then she adds, "But I'm a little butterball." At 110 pounds, that's an outright lie.

When the selection announcement was made, Rhea says, "I was very excited, extremely surprised, knowing the competition, having met some absolutely fantastic people with the interview group I was with. I guess none of us will ever know why some of us were selected and others didn't make it. Everyone seemed eminently qualified." Yet she added, "I guess we are all kind of used to not being ordinary.

"I notice that the women chosen are all very successful in their fields without being militant women's libbers or overly masculine. We're ladylike—well-mannered, if you like."

Dr. Seddon has in mind to examine the effects of space travel on female metabolism. "In space," she says, "the myth that women's monthly hormonal cycles make them unfit to be astronauts or presidents will either be proven or put to rest. I want to find out the answers to questions like: will women be more emotional than men in space? Can we handle danger?"

Is she frightened? "Personally no, not yet. Professionally, a little. The nightmare is not in dying. It's the thought of not performing well that bothers me."

It is true the sudden attention and publicity has changed her. "I feel the burden to succeed especially because of other women who want to go into the space program. They will be looking to us to do well so that NASA will accept more women in the future."

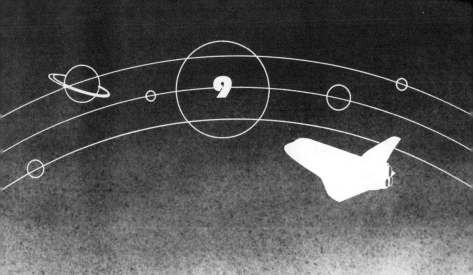

SHANNON LUCID

Shannon Lucid's life already reads like an adventure novel with a suspenseful ending of each chapter. When she was only six weeks old, she and her Baptist missionary parents, Oscar and Rachel Wells, were taken prisoner in Shanghai by the invading Japanese army.

Luckily, they were among the first to be released under a prisoner exchange program. Shan-

non and her parents were able to come back to the United States when she was a year old. The family returned to China after World War II to continue their work, only to be expelled by the Communists in 1949.

Shannon still remembers some of the highlights of this eventful childhood. One of the most memorable events was bouncing over Chinese mountain passes in a vintage DC-3, looking down on the world below her. She sat with her face pressed against the window, chattering away with all the enthusiasm of a very excited five-year-old. From then on, she dreamed of being a pilot.

Space travel was also in her plans. Later, when growing up in Bethany, Oklahoma, a suburb of Oklahoma City, she wrote an eighth-grade paper on rocket research. She prefaced her theme with this statement, "If the science shortage is in such dire status as they claim, they'd let women in on the same ground as men."

She set about planning her life to test that claim. After graduating from high school in 1960, Shannon entered Wheaton College in Illinois as a chemistry major.

Why chemistry? "When I was in grade school," she remembers, "someone told me that water is composed of hydrogen and oxygen. That seemed to me the most amazing thing, that gases could be liquid. I just couldn't imagine how any human could figure that out. Then someone said that a chemist was a type of person who did that sort of thing. So I decided I'd also like to be able to do something like that. They also told me, if you're going to be a chemist, you have to know math. That almost dissuaded me, because I wasn't really good in arithmetic when I was young."

That didn't stop her. It just meant she had to spend a few more hours on that subject, whether she liked it or not. As she began to understand the mystery of figures, she wondered why she had ever hated arithmetic. It has been a good lesson throughout her life. Finding out why she doesn't like something, or even someone, is the first step in making a change.

"Wheaton was really a good school," she says, "and I got a good chemistry background there."

She was on a strict budget and had to earn all her living expenses. She worked in the dining room at the student union. There may also be a few home owners in Wheaton, Illinois who will read about their former cleaning lady in outer space, for that was another job Shannon took on.

"After two years," she says, "I ran out of money. They upped the tuition quite dramatically, and I just couldn't make it."

She transferred to the University of Oklahoma in Norman where she received a B.S. in chemistry in 1963. She still hadn't forgotten her dream as a five-year-old—to become a pilot. She began taking flying lessons, paying for them with odd jobs around the airfield. She could soon count herself a real pro.

Shannon has already logged more than 2,000 hours of commercial, instrument, and multi-engine flying time. She wanted to be a commercial pilot in the mid-sixties. She applied for jobs all over the country, but, she says, "I was ten years too early for women in flying. I used to tell myself that I only wanted the job because I was qualified, not because I was a woman." She pauses for a chuckle. "Then, after a while, I began to wonder whether it might not be nice to be somebody's token woman."

That's not the real Lucid talking. She's quick to point out, "I'd rather not be thought of as a woman doing something unusual. I'm just a person doing it."

This is the quote to take seriously, for she never relied on any advantage to being a woman; conversely, her career has always been an uphill fight.

After graduation, Shannon spent a year as a teaching assistant at Oklahoma and two years as a senior technician at the Oklahoma Medical Research Foundation. In 1966 she got a job at Kerr-McGee Corporation's technical center in Oklahoma City.

"I did a little bit of everything," she says. "Then I got promoted to the chemistry department and worked in fertilizers."

Ironically, Shannon met her husband, Mike Lucid, when he rejected her for a job there. "I thought she was overqualified," he explains. But he remembered the bright upbeat outlook about her life and her determination to accomplish just what she set out to do. Later, when there was a more challenging job opening, she was the first one he called.

He also started calling after working hours. They discovered they shared many interests, and soon they were setting their wedding date. That was in 1967, and a year later their first daughter was born. She was named Kawai.

"In those days they'd only let you work up to seven months when you were having a baby." She was disappointed when someone was trained immediately to take over her job.

At home she was busy, but she missed the challenge of a career. Would motherhood put an end to all that? "Mike suggested I go to graduate school, so I did. I went into biochemistry because, well, it was here, where I could arrange transportation and babysitting."

Another daughter, Shandra, was born in 1970. Shannon went on to earn a Ph.D. in biochemistry with a minor in physical chemistry. "It just means that I am looking at the chemistry of living organisms," she explains.

In 1973 their third child, Michael, was born. Shannon continued her work at the University of Oklahoma where she was carrying on experiments in researching the effects of carcinogens on laboratory rats. She remembers life wasn't all that easy, even with a helpful husband to share the job of raising a young family. Yet she managed to balance her priorities. She saved time for family and PTA. It was challenging work that made the effort worthwhile.

With her degree in hand, she expected to continue her research work and live the ordinary—well, almost ordinary—life of a suburban housewife. But on the horizon another challenge presented itself.

"I've always been a space nut," she admits, so when she heard NASA's call, she longed to reach for the sky. She talked it over with her family. No one took her too seriously. She was approaching middle age. She had three children. Her research had nothing to do, she thought, with matters of outer space. But what did she have to lose?

She mailed her application. She was delightfully surprised when she made the first cut, and dumbfounded when the magic word came from George Abbey that she was one of the chosen six.

Her husband Mike was terribly proud. They had already discussed what would happen if she were selected. He'd have to look for a job in Houston if the family were to stay together. There was no doubt of that, and with his technical background he'd have little trouble finding a position.

The older girls were excited about having an astronaut for a mother, but they weren't all that enthusiastic about going to Houston.

"I think moving a few times is good," Shannon explains. "If you get stuck in one place, it's harder to change when you get older."

She was right. The move went smoothly. The family soon settled in, and friends were made easily. Shannon herself had the hardest job of adjusting to an entirely new schedule that was rarely on a nine-to-five timetable. There was a certain amount of travel right at the beginning, but everyone pitched in to smooth the way.

Mom is a special drawing card at the local PTA

meetings, although Shannon is extremely modest about her career, honestly surprised she's caused so much notice.

There are times when Shannon gets a bit impatient with reporters who keep asking about how she manages to have a family life with her busy schedule. Her answer is, "We do the same work as the men, yet nobody asks them about how their kids feel about their work."

Shannon is the oldest of the women astronauts, born in 1943, "more mature in a lot of ways than anyone I know," says a friend. "She's a strong person you just turn to naturally for advice. Maybe it's her missionary background, but she can make you feel nothing is unsolvable, and she does it without giving you a sermon."

She's also the tallest of the women, lacking one inch of being a six-footer. She is the first chemist to join the astronaut corps too.

Shannon's advice for anyone wanting to follow in her footsteps is to select her own field of interest, preferably science. "Do it well, to the best of your ability. We'll be needing all types of people."

Although Shannon has a strong record of achievement and has never been reticent about shaking up the establishment to make things happen, she is a surprisingly patient, quiet person.

Shannon hopes sometime soon she'll be saying goodbye to her family for a short trip in space. "Wouldn't it be great when I'm old and gray," she muses, "to be able to lean back in my rocking chair and remember when I was taking a stroll among the stars."

Being more practical, she laughs a deep chuckle. "Get to thinking about how your work could benefit from a zero-gravity, high-vacuum environment. Then buy some space on the Shuttle and keep my job going."

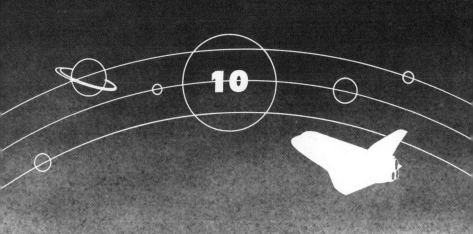

KATHRYN
SULLIVAN

It seems only fitting that Kathryn Sullivan should be the first woman to walk in space. She's been studying satellite maps of our Earth since the days they were available for research scientists. Her own special field is geology, particularly marine geology. Her doctoral thesis concerned the structure and evolution of the continental shelf and deep-sea floor east of the Grand Banks of Newfoundland.

Until our space age could track and analyze whole sections of topography from above, our knowledge of underseascapes was limited to figures taken in a painstakingly slow process of recording successive sonar counts. There were other sources of study too. Sediments from the ocean floor were "mined" and analyzed. Kathy has been involved in all of them, but she kept thinking it would be great fun to float free up there in outer space, looking back at the world she was trying to map and understand.

In her very first interview after having been chosen as an astronaut candidate, she admitted, "The part I am really looking forward to is the EVA (Extra Vehicular Activity), walking in space. Since I am an earth scientist, the idea of being able to look back at Earth in orbit is truly exciting to me. I'd also love to do more space exploration. I wouldn't mind trying Mars," she added with a laugh. "What a landscape."

Because she is the youngest of the astronauts in training, she may get there. She was twenty-six when she was chosen in 1978.

Kathy was born in New Jersey, but her family soon moved to Woodland Hills, California. She is an excellent athlete. Raised as a Christian Scientist, she neither smokes nor drinks.

"I have no special program for staying fit," Kathy admits, "but I'm pretty athletic and basically healthy. I run, play racquetball, enjoy competitive sailing and generally stay in motion as much as possible." She's even tried ice hockey as a sport.

Has she always thought about being an astronaut? "Always," she says very definitely. "At least since the moon landings."

But how to train for it? Her father, an aeronautical engineer, and her brother, a jet pilot, had more of a shot at it, she thought, so she just continued on with the work she liked best. Her "field assignments," which included research aboard ship, were exciting and actually proved to be very good background for an astronaut.

"I've had experience on board ship working on experiments, which I imagine is not unlike the space Shuttle, working at close quarters with people, in isolation," she says.

She's had to monitor life-support systems on shipboard, and she has also been trained in navigation and radio communication.

"Being 500 miles at sea is very similar to a space mission. You'd better have everything you need and plans for every contingency."

But Kathy laughingly admits things are planned a bit more thoroughly at NASA. "On marine expeditions it was easier to say, 'Throw it aboard; it's close enough; let's go.' Here that freewheeling is not permissible. You work everything down to the wire. It's a level of discipline I'm striving to improve."

Her training started with an earth science degree from the University of California, Santa Cruz. She spent one year as an undergraduate exchange student at the University of Bergen in Norway.

Kathy is a very outgoing person. It's important to her to communicate with people. If it meant learning a new language, she set about doing just that. By the time she had graduated from college she had mastered six languages.

"I'd never say mastered," Kathy corrects, "but I can get by without too much trouble. Some of the Nordic dialects are hard to pronounce though."

Her doctorate in geophysics was earned at Dalhousie University in Halifax, Nova Scotia. She has also taken part in a number of oceanographic expeditions under the auspices of the U.S. Geological Survey and the Woods Hole Oceanographic Institute.

Kathryn Sullivan is no token woman for the astronaut corps, and she hopes that none of her fellow women colleagues are ever accused of such a thing. "I believe NASA chose qualified people," Kathy says. "I wouldn't want to slip in just because I'm a woman. We're putting people's lives, reputations, and a lot of money into hands we'd better trust."

The astronauts themselves are not in it for the glory or money. Times have changed. There are no lucrative *Life* magazine contracts, no free life insurance packages that were presented to the original seven astronauts.

"In the early days, NASA was a very new agency," Kathy explains. "No rules were written that governed what an astronaut could or could not accept. This was a whole new ball game. The ball game has subsequently been institutionalized, and we are all now well-signed and well-trained civil servants. And if somebody comes up and offers you a Corvette, unless it's a three-inch plastic model that costs forty-nine cents, you'd better not take it."

When asked what's important to her about going up in space, she repeats what many of the astronauts have said. "It's important for man to have frontiers, to explore and callenge himself. One of the great pluses is that it brings the best people in the world together to break out of formal limitations. The unity it generates is a very good thing."

But she says it didn't really bother her not to be the first woman in space. Having an assignment down the line suits her fine. "Then I'll be less famous and can return to scientific work more quickly."

Kathy is a member of the Sierra Club and ardently concerned about the earth and oceans she has been studying. "I don't want to be an astronaut just because we mucked up down here and need to run away from the mess. Space exploration works as long as it's not a substitute for taking care of the Earth."

Kathy knows she still has a lot of training ahead of her. Even a knowledge of six languages may not be enough. She'll have to learn space talk, not for conversing with extraterrestrials, but that technical, cool, unemotional jargon that communicates all the scientific readouts from space to Earth. It may be the most important language of the future.

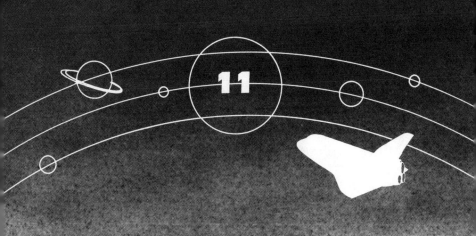

ANNA FISHER

Anna Fisher is described by many of her coworkers
as "just a doll." This is not a slur womens libbers
should take to heart. It means she's a cooperative,
friendly, unaffected person who can take on other's
problems as well as her own.

Because she does have that pert, wholesome
look, she has been one of the photographers' favor-
ites. She suffered through many an inane interview,

fielding silly questions, trying to divert attention to the space research itself.

Anna is very serious about her role for the future. "Mankind needs something to dream about. We've explored our world very thoroughly. The only frontiers left are the ocean and outer space. I want to be a part of that."

Anna decided when she was in the seventh grade that she wanted to be an astronaut. That was when her hero, Commander Alan Shepard, shot his way into space in his Mercury capsule over the Atlantic. "But it was such a preposterous thought that I could do something like that myself, and I knew people would laugh, so I didn't talk about it."

When she wasn't dreaming of outer space, she practiced ballet and gymnastics. "It's really a great way to help coordination and keep the body flexible," she explains.

She had natural talent, but it was the disciplined hours of practice that made her excel in both.

She found time to enjoy team sports in school. Competition sharpened the goal to win. With three younger brothers, she's even managed to be included in games of touch football and softball. Small-boned, almost fragile, it had to be speed and coordination that kept her out of trouble.

Anna has never felt a problem competing with men. She remembers during medical school "a bunch of us started to play co-ed water polo. It was fun because men and women could play with and against each other."

Science was her favorite school subject. Chemistry was her major at UCLA. She deliberately chose to go into medicine, "because I thought it would be the best qualification to have if I ever had a chance to be an astronaut."

Anna met her husband, Bill Fisher, while they were medical students. They both specialized in emergency medicine. It is an emerging field in its own right. It takes a cool head and competency in many fields to handle it all. Patient load often ran as high as sixty cases a shift.

Bill and Anna Fisher have more than their profession in common. Their free time, whenever they can juggle schedules, is almost always taken up in sports. They are obviously not spectators. "We never watch what we can do."

They play a fiercely competitive game of tennis. They both love skiing and backpacking in the mountains near Los Angeles. Scuba diving is their newest hobby. Anna's eyes light up when she talks about the beauty of undersea life, the thrill and satisfaction of relating to a totally new kind of environment. To her, the rewards of risk-taking always outweigh the potential dangers of fear of the unknown.

Two weeks after Anna and Bill were married, they got wind of NASA's search for qualified astronaut candidates. Both applied. What could they do to prepare themselves?

They believe strongly that running is the most efficient way to improve body conditioning. To psych themselves up, Anna says with a giggle, "Bill went out and bought themes from *Rocky* and *Star Wars* on cassettes. We listened to them and we ran every day."

They worked out as a team, but Anna was the first to be chosen.

"Yes, it was a disappointment for him, but he was very happy for me. I think I was selected first because I had a degree in chemisty before I ever went into medicine," she says.

Dr. Carolyn Huntoon, a NASA biochemist and the one woman on the selection panel, agrees. "What we were looking for, first of all, was a strong academic background. But we also searched for people who had taken that background and done something with it. Dr. Fisher diversified. In other words, we wanted someone technically competent, with an advanced degree, and yet someone who could still learn new things."

On their first Christmas in Houston, Bill gave Anna a plaque that read, "The best man for the job may be a woman."

Three years later, Dr. Bill Fisher became an astronaut candidate himself.

"He's always been very proud and supportive," says Anna, "and now it's even better that he has joined the corps. I'm glad I have him to talk everything over with."

With all her accomplishments, Anna admits she tends to depend on her husband in an old-fashioned way. "I don't know if that means I'm weak or just human," she says, "but I need that. I feel very, very lucky to have a husband I love and who loves me, and to be a doctor—and when I think now I'm an astronaut too, it's just incredible. A fairy tale.

"We know we'll always be involved in the space program. We both consider it such an honor and a challenge. I don't think it mattered that much to us who got there first."

Having a family was an important part of their future plans. Daughter Kirstin Ann was born in 1983. Mom was back on her job right away, but the proud parents are juggling their schedules so there'll be a Fisher on hand, and not a babysitter, as much as possible.

Anna sees her job as a special challenge. "There will obviously be a need for men and women trained in emergency medicine. In my lifetime, maybe in the next fifty years, there will be space stations, big ones. Accidents will happen. We'll need to know how to stabilize a patient in zero G environment. It's a whole new area. We have a lot to learn."

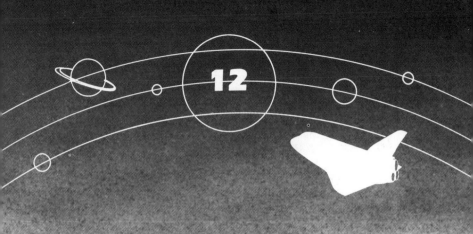

MARY CLEAVE

Mary Cleave—she's tiny and she's impish, taking her job very seriously, but bubbling over with earthy, outrageous humor at any moment.

Part of that humor stems from her job and training as a sanitary engineer. Everybody makes jokes about it, and she does too, remembering that her mother taught her to read at the age of two while she was sitting on the potty. Ever since, Mary insists she has associated toilet training with higher education.

Mary's mother was a high school biology teacher on Long Island, the third generation of the family to be naturalists. Mary's father is a musician, trumpet player and conductor. He looks a little like Toscanini with wild tousled hair.

There was never a great deal of money to indulge three growing daughters, but no one seemed to mind. Mary is the middle child. The Cleaves operated a summer camp on Lake Champlain in the Adirondacks. It was there that Mary saw firsthand what could happen to a crystal-pure body of water polluted by human indifference to the disposal of sewage and industrial waste. Somebody had to care about what was happening. Mary did, but there wasn't much she could do about it then.

Flying—at least the thought of flying—was a consuming passion of hers at a very early age. By the time she was ten she had assembled every model plane she could get her hands on.

Mary grew up a tomboy, she admits. "My sister says it's a personality type. 'You always have to have one foot over the edge.' I was born that way."

She remembers one Armed Forces Day when her parents took her to an air show at an Air Force base. She was in heaven. She could actually climb into the cockpit of one of the jets on display.

"Boy, I'd like to fly one of these babies," she remembers saying. She also remembers the answer. "You'll never fly one of these, young lady."

It was a statement she swore she'd prove wrong, but young ladies weren't accepted as fighter pilots at the time, and fighting wasn't what Mary wanted to do with that plane, anyway.

Saving every penny she could earn from odd jobs and allowance and with the generous help of understanding parents, Mary's dream of flying came true. She had her pilot's license before she was old enough to operate a car.

"I would drive her to the airport in our car," her mother says, "and then she would take me for a ride in the plane."

There weren't many others she could tempt as passengers, probably because the sight of the pilot arriving at the field with two pillows under her arm didn't inspire confidence. She sat on one cushion and shoved the other behind her back so she could reach the controls.

If only she could grow faster, she thought. She tried dangling upside down from the top of a door in ski boots, hoping to stretch an inch of growth. Nothing helped. Her adult height is still a diminutive 5 feet 1½ inches, half an inch short even for the airlines' minimum regulations for female flight attendants.

When asked recently if she'd always been interested in space beyond the limits of normal flight travel, Mary answered with a grin, "Well, one of my favorite books was a novel by Robert Heinlein, entitled *Space Cadet*."

Yet even though she'd grown up in a generation where rocket travel was described in newspaper headlines as well as in books of fiction, she'd never really thought she would have that option. There were plenty of other useful things she wanted to try earthbound. She loved the out-of-doors. She was a born naturalist, taking notes, tracking wildlife. Her interests spread in many fields.

"I'm just sort of bumping through life," she admits, "like it was bumper cars. You know, just going around aiming and then, wham, being spit out over there."

By the time she was eighteen she was desperate for a change of scenery and adventure beyond the home front. Skiing was a favorite sport, and skiing and Colorado went together. She chose to attend Colorado State University.

Mary started with the idea of becoming a veterinarian. After two years she realized she was just too small to be a large animal vet. Her arms weren't long enough. She switched to biology with the idea of following a teaching career similar to her mother's.

Mary always seems to have a way of making life an adventure, even in the not so unusual job of teaching. She was hired as a tutor aboard a ship, a "floating campus," where she taught college kids biology as they sailed from port to port. Her interest in ecology and pollution control grew as she saw the devastating effects of civilization around the world. She took samples of water wherever she went and kept records of their analyses.

In 1971 she went back to school with a definite goal in mind. She entered Utah State University, where she specialized in phycology, the study of algae. "But I gave up telling anyone what I did in those terms," she laughs. "They just thought I had a lisp and right away started telling me about their nervous breakdowns."

She worked in the Utah Water Research Laboratory. Most of the men in the lab were certified engineers. She could see that if she were really serious about wanting to have a part in cleaning up the environment, she'd have to get a doctorate in either civil or environmental engineering. She couldn't choose between the two, so she earned both degrees, the first woman to do so at Utah State.

She admits it was an unusual career for a woman. She traveled between labs and sewers. She compares her profession of "sewer worker" to being a mortician. "They always border on being off-limits to society, and after a while they start to look the part—you know, tattoos, motorcycles, dirty fingernails. They look like they're right out of the fifties."

Mary was the only woman in her inspection crew. She met a wall of resentment. Most of her colleagues were Mormons, who had their own circumscribed views as to what was an appropriate job for a woman.

Mary was not discouraged. She had always been a bit of a maverick. She rode her own motorcycle for pleasure. She dressed in jeans and boots. She was little, but she had a lot of nerve. She could take kidding and she could dish it right back. She began to be accepted, and her hard work and superior intelligence earned respect.

She first heard about NASA's call for astronaut

candidates back in '78 when she was still working on her degree. One of her friends handed her an application form, saying she was probably the only engineer in the lab crazy enough to try for it.

It sounded like a good idea. Someone should start thinking about the future, thinking about how to keep a clean, pure environment for future generations who were bound to start colonizing outer space. We'd done a poor job on earth as we multiplied, Mary told herself. There might be a chance to start space pioneers on the right course. Pioneer—Mary wanted to fit that word.

She filled out all the proper forms. She was more worried that her small physical stature, rather than her academic training, would eliminate her from the competition. But aboard a space vehicle without gravity to require strength, smallness of size and weight is an advantage. She hoped they'd remember that.

Almost by return mail she received a postal card, "Thanks, but no thanks." Polite but final. She had no idea why she had been turned down, but she knew it had been a long shot in the first place.

Mary was delighted, however, that six women were chosen as astronauts. At least they'd broken the sex barrier. Maybe she'd have another chance.

Two years later she did. The call from NASA for applicants was issued again. She filled out the same forms and mailed them.

This time she didn't receive that return postal. She knew she'd made the first cut because government investigators dropped by her small hometown of Wellsville, Utah, to make discreet inquiries about the character of one Mary Cleave. Her neighbors couldn't quite figure out why the feds were interested in her.

The next official word was an invitation to come to Houston for interviews. Her surprised fellow workers in the Sanitation Department stopped laughing. Only Mary took it less seriously. At least she'd get a chance to see the Space Center on a specially escorted tour. That would be worth the trip. There would be no disappointment, no misty eyes, no matter what the outcome. This was to be a fun experience.

Mary had mixed feelings when she arrived at the NASA complex outside of Houston. The stark white concrete buildings with their black-tinted glass windows looked austere, like a college campus without the ivy and without any undergraduates. She could get used to that, but it was the presence of the military that made her uneasy. She was the product of the days of student revolt and antiwar sentiment.

I've always had trouble with authority figures," she admits.

NASA is quick to assert that it is a civilian agency, but most of the male astronauts are high-ranking military officers. Their dress code, even when not in uniform, tended to be starched and conservative. Mary wasn't sure whether her waist-length hair, corduroys, and earth shoes would quite fit in. She was not one for making changes to fit a mold.

Each group of astronauts went through a series of tests and interviews that lasted from Monday through Friday. A thorough physical came first: blood samples, urine samples, endurance tests; there was no room for health problems in zero gravity.

Then there were lectures on what the work of an astronaut was all about. It was a reverse selling job. Anyone expecting to further a career in a particular field should step back and have second thoughts. "Someone who wants to do research and is doing very well in his field," George Abbey said, "will have to accept the fact that as an astronaut he or she will be implementing someone else's experiments, not his own."

Then there was the scary part of being told all of the things that might happen on a space flight that could bring instant death, or worse. There's no way to parachute out of the Space Shuttle, and there are only two pressurized space suits on board at any time. If a rescue ship is able to rendezvous with a crippled orbiter, crew members might be transported through the vacuum of space by being tucked into inflatable balloons called personal rescue enclosures, fabric spheres, 30 inches (76 centimeters) in diameter.

Each applicant was asked to experience a rehearsal of just such a maneuver. Their watches were removed. Then they were told to crawl into one of the escape balls which was zipped up after them. They had no idea how long they were expected to stay inside the blackness.

The experiment lasted only fifteen minutes, but there were some candidates who panicked and tried to rip open their balloon. Mary was much smaller than the others and therefore didn't experience quite the same discomfort. She surprised everyone by simply curling up and going to sleep.

Mary still had to meet the two psychiatrists. No one had told her about the Mr. Good and Mr. Bad Guy approaches. When she met the gruff, impatient one, she simply called his bluff. "I thought psychiatrists were supposed to be nice and understanding. What's wrong with you?"

She took him so much by surprise, he laughed. He'd met the unflappable candidate. He was friendly from then on.

One of the questions asked everyone was, "If you were to die and come back as something other than a human, what would that be?"

There were plenty of strange answers, but it took Mary only a moment of thought to answer, "A sea gull, a good practical bird. He cleans up a lot of things. I remember when I was working on a ship, I used to feed them off the fantail."

Another question the committee asked, more out of curiosity than for relevance in selection, was how long each applicant had wanted to be an astronaut.

There were many who answered, "Always," digging up memories from childhood to explain how this dream had dominated their entire lives.

Mary just chuckled. "Are you serious? I'm a pragmatist. I thought you guys would never take women into the program."

Then it was back to Utah. She'd had the grand tour. It had been fun. She had no expectations that she would be called back, not after meeting so many other great people, all qualifed for those few spots in the elite group of "space cadets."

But the word came on May 28. "Mary, I think we've had enough time to make our decision. If you're still interested, we'd like to have you join us."

Her first word was not "Yes." The words were, "Who is this?" She was sure someone was kidding her. When she found out she was talking with George Abbey himself, the excited answer came back loud and clear, "Yes, oh, yes."

Two months later she arrived in Houston for good. It took her three days to drive from Utah, pulling a 24-foot U-Haul trailer. She had been living in a huge old farmhouse with a spectacular view of the mountains. House and view had come with a price tag of $12,500. She wasn't prepared for the Houston shock. The city had been exploding in size, unable to keep pace with the housing demand.

"When I look up I like to see land," Mary said, "but Houston is so flat, you can never see anything except sky. I told my realtor if I couldn't look at mountains I'd have to look at the ocean."

She finally settled for a small cottage set on stilts on the shores of Galveston Bay. It cost her $69,000. She had sea gulls and herons to keep her company.

During working hours her immediate company consisted of two fellow astronauts, Lieutenant Commander Michael Coats of the Navy and Major Richard Mullane of the Air Force, who were assigned shared duties and a tiny office space. Before she met her colleagues she took a deep breath and crossed her fingers. She'd have to learn to cope with military brass. She didn't know what to expect.

Neither did Coats or Mullane. They agreed to treat their new office-mate just as if she were a plebe. When Mary walked into her office for the first time, every bit of furniture was stacked on top of her desk, and the desk was shoved behind a bank of filing cabinets.

"Okay, you guys," she said, "you asked for it. The first thing we're going to do is to get rid of this junky government furniture. I'm going to decorate this place in French Provincial. And as soon as you get the floor cleaned up I'm going to put down a mauve rug. Yeah, that'd be nice."

The ice was broken. The only decorating changes actually made were the hanging of her favorite cartoon by Gahan Wilson, showing two characters in gas masks standing in an office. One of them says, "I'm sorry, Senator. It's some more of those crackpot conservationists." She also put up a picture of her father conducting the symphony orchestra.

Mary was here to stay. NASA would have to cope.

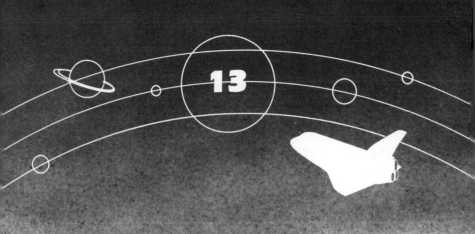

BONNIE DUNBAR

"Mercury, Gemini, Apollo, and Skylab were a Lewis and Clark kind of thing," explains a NASA spokesman. "Now we're sending up settlers. The Shuttle is the new Conestoga wagon."

Bonnie Dunbar's parents didn't exactly come to the state of Washington in a covered wagon, but they still fit the picture of pioneers, who must be just a bit amazed at their daughter's pioneering plans. Bonnie describes her family.

"My parents are phenomenal," she says. "The farm I grew up on in eastern Washington had been barren land until 1948, when my mom and dad homesteaded there. They built a wood frame tent that my mother lived in most of the time when my dad was doing wheat farming in northern Oregon. . . . There are still tree houses there that I built.

"I was part of the 1949 baby boom that came along at the time the first sputnik was launched. I was the oldest of four kids," she explains, "and we were very isolated from the nearest town, so I grew up as a bookworm and lived in a very imaginary world. I read a lot of science fiction and a lot of the old classics too."

She feels this rather special upbringing gave her a background of self-reliance. Her parents always told her, "Do what you want; if it's really worth it to you, then persevere."

"My folks never steered me," she says, "but they maintained that the only limitations you have are in your mind. We didn't have any college graduates in our family, and because I was the oldest, my mother made me swear I wouldn't get married until I had a college degree. She thought that was important."

Bonnie was a good student in both science and literature, but it was a high school physics teacher who encouraged her to major in engineering and to continue reading as a pastime.

"I considered MIT, but it was too expensive, and I also thought of Cal Tech, until someone sent me a very nice letter telling me they didn't have any coeducational dormitories, which was another way of saying that they weren't academically coeducational."

Fate seems to have taken a hand in the following decision to enroll at the University of Washington. This was the school that had just been commissioned to help develop the heat shield for the space shuttle. Bonnie was in on the earliest research that produced the ceramic tiles that would be used to protect Columbia from the temperature extremes during Earth re-entry.

People still confuse her technical expertise and her degree as a ceramic engineer with the art of making clay pots. She doesn't bother to tell them her master's thesis was in the field of mechanisms and kinetics of ionic diffusion in sodium beta-alumina.

"I loved science, and I was always interested in the space program," she says. "My generation grew up with space flight as part of the environment. So I could see myself as a jet pilot, a scientist—even flying a spacecraft. I was a bit of a dreamer," she admits. But few people knew she had hopes of traveling in that vehicle she was helping to protect.

"When you go to school and pick out a major, you don't say, 'I'm going to be an astronaut.' The only person I told at that time was the head of the department because I knew he wouldn't consider me absolutely bonkers."

When she was a kid, she can remember sleeping out on haystacks at the farm, looking up at the stars and thinking about being "out there."

"I didn't define it as wanting to be an astronaut,

but I do remember at one point that I wanted to be a jet pilot. I used to watch the television station sign off at night with a picture of a jet going through the clouds, and I guess I was sort of naive about it. I didn't realize that women weren't jet pilots."

Bonnie didn't wait around idly for NASA to knock on her door. After graduating cum laude from the University of Washington in 1971, she worked for Boeing Computer Services for two years as a systems analyst, then returned to the university for graduate work in her field of ceramics.

In 1975 she was invited to participate in research at Hartwell Laboratories in Oxford, England. She then accepted a job at Rockwell International, helping to set up production facilities in California for the tiles to be used on the Shuttle. She also made some personal contacts at NASA, so she'd be the first to know when they were going to hire new astronauts.

When the call went out in 1978 she was one of the first to apply. She made it through to the finals but was dropped in the last elimination. She was more determined than ever to try again.

"In looking over the resumes of those who'd been accepted, I realized that they had a lot of interests and worked in a number of different disciplines," Bonnie said. "I could see that I needed to enlarge my background and improve myself. I was twenty-nine by then, and I was at the point where I was feeling I didn't want to be known as the tile expert all my life." She set about making a change.

"When I'd been in Houston for interviews for the astronaut program, I'd been offered several jobs at the Johnson Space Center, and I decided there were interesting possibilities in flight operations there. So I went from being a senior research engineer, working in a lab with materials, to being a systems engineer, working in an office with people."

She also represented Rockwell International as a member of the Dr. Kraft Ehricke evaluation committee on ways to use outer space for industrial purposes. It was a way to put her imagination to practical use.

Two years later, when she applied for the astronaut class of 1980, she was accepted. "I just moved my office from one side of the building to another," she says with a laugh.

She's very hopeful there will be many other women who will qualify for space work. "The reason so few women are selected is that you have to have a science or engineering background. When I started my education, only 3 percent of the engineering students were women, and now the proportion is up to 15 or 20 percent. So we're really beginning to see some growth. But what I respect NASA for is not making the requirements any different for women."

Her conversation often turns to dissipating velocity and synthesizing gravity, but she sprinkles the professional jargon with an occasional "Wow" and "By golly."

That "Wow" is a pretty apt description of what

she sees for the future. Bonnie Dunbar claims that the U.S. space program is a tremendous boost for the country's technology and economy.

"As we developed cars, railroads, and airplanes," she points out, "we needed gas stations and air terminals. What we need now is a space station. What we call Space Operations Center would allow us to do some of the best observations of weather, crops, and oceans, as well as material processing and service repair of vehicles. It's going to happen . . . and it's certainly not going to help us economically to ask either the Japanese or the Europeans to launch our satellites for us."

Bonnie also talks about building furnaces in space that can manufacture new alloys and crystals. Bonnie has come a long way from the haystacks, but she's still looking at the stars.

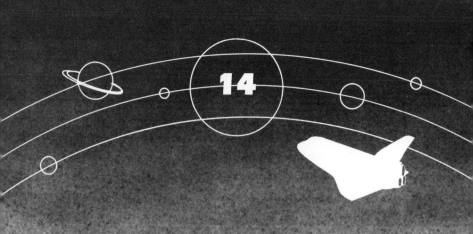

ASTRONAUT CANDIDATES

Turn south from the glass towers of Houston and you'll be on the freeway heading toward Galveston Bay. You pass a stretch of used car lots and bargain warehouse outlets. It's flat country, and depending on the season of the year, it's either hot and humid or cold and clammy, just about like a laundromat, one resident with a sense of humor remarked. But you're in the neighborhood of some pretty exciting happenings.

The signs overhead point to the turnoff for the Lyndon B. Johnson Space Center. It is located in Clear Lake City, an instant suburb of Houston. Nothing was here twenty-five years ago.

Before you ever get to the main gate of the Center, you'll see on your left a very impressive display of obsolete rocketry. Some are pointing toward the sky, others are stretched out on the ground as if aimed for the highway traffic that speeds by a few hundred feet away.

The firing mechanisms of the space vehicles are monstrously large, but the capsules that housed early space travelers look like fiendishly contrived torture chambers.

There's more inside the space museum for tourists to see, but the arriving astronaut candidates (that's what they are called for the first year of their training) have had the tour before and they are ready to report in. Every one of them admits to a feeling of excitement that they are to be part of this very special world, planning unheard of things for the future.

When the first seven male space men (they weren't designated astronauts in 1959) arrived in Houston, they were already celebrities. Their names were household words. They were officers of the elite military air force, arriving in sleek cars.

Times have changed. The close-knit cadre of test pilots has disappeared, now that having "the right stuff" most probably means being able to solve quadratic equations in their heads. There are still a lot of top brass military men around, but uniforms are not worn, and there's no snapping to attention.

Six of the astronaut candidates in 1978. Left to right: Margaret (Rhea) Seddon, Anna Fisher, Judith Resnik, Shannon Lucid, Sally Ride, and Kathryn Sullivan.

The new class of 1978 arrived one at a time, some in old cars, a few in shiny recent models, some in taxis. There didn't seem to be any standard code of appearance, either. The women are strikingly individual. The tallest, a biochemist and mother of three, is five foot eleven; the shortest, a mere five foot two, weighing in at 98 pounds. The one trait they all share and which they were soon to prove is that they are all hard workers and achievers.

"The most recent astronaut groups are generally fairly quiet, unassuming people," one Johnson Space Center public information officer commented. "Maybe it's just that the whole space program has matured enough so that we can now settle down to the business of space flight."

The Space Center itself is a group of white concrete-and-glass buildings scattered over a well-kept campus. This isn't the climate or atmosphere for ivy-clad bell towers. It is better considered a well designed factory for scientists searching for answers in outer space.

The first job of the astronauts after checking in was to find a place to live, preferably close to the base. Housing has not kept pace with demand. Some of the women were amazed at the price of stark quarters, but luxuries had never been promised.

Few grumbles were heard. They knew if ever they were to drop out of the program, there were hundreds of willing applicants to take their place. And it had been made very clear that the government had no intention of investing about ten million dollars in their future if they weren't going to make this their life's work. This is the estimated figure it costs to train and maintain an astronaut during his or her career at NASA.

Although military uniforms had long ago disappeared, certain clothing was provided for the as-

The astronauts at water-survival training in 1978. Here they are taking a break from various training exercises. Left to right: Ride, Resnik, Fisher, Sullivan, and Seddon.

Ride chooses a jacket to complete her set of Shuttle constant-wear overalls.

tronauts, with no regulation as to when it had to be worn. There were comfortable collared tee shirts and slacks for both men and women. A sort of army-type fatigue was issued for rougher work, but it came in light blue, gray green, or drab orange. A specially designed patch designated their rank of astronaut candidate. Plenty of extra pockets and zippered compartments were stitched in to get them used to keeping instruments and tools they'd need in their flight suits. Finally, each of them was fitted with the neat pleated suit they would be wearing aboard the Shuttle, fireproof and adjustable for changes of posture in space.

These were the outfits worn in the first picture-taking. The new class of astronauts did command plenty of press coverage, principally because it was the first time women had been selected for the job. Each of them posed for individual portraits in their new NASA wardrobe. One-to-one interviews were taped on video film, and then the press was invited to meet them in the public relations building of the Space Center.

It is a rather small room with a raised dais at one end. Microphones are placed all along a table. Lights are trained on those being interviewed, for this again will be taped and put on film. The questions seemed endless and repetitious.

NASA tried to cooperate with the news media, yet shield their proteges until they'd had time to adjust to their new public role. They were all made to realize that good public relations for the space program meant more adequate funding for their future training. Once the press had had their day, it was time to settle down to more serious business.

George Abbey, who had had the final voice in their selection, gave them all a welcoming speech. He repeated what they had been told when they had first come as finalists to the Space Center. He explained that they all had to be team players. "People set on doing their own thing, no matter how bright, probably won't be happy here."

There would be no room for people who couldn't accept instruction. "Scientists have to understand that they will be performing other people's experiments, not their own."

Next came assignments. The women had no opportunity to band together. "George Abbey was very careful about that in assigning office space and so on," Sally Ride explained.

Over the next few weeks the women became friends, "but not really close friends," one of them said. Yet there were times when the original six were brought together for meetings.

"We got together to chat about certain issues that might come up. We decided if there were issues that would have relevance to future women in space, we would discuss them and have a good position on them."

There were obvious bits of advice they could give NASA on flight equipment. Two-piece suits were suggested. Skin softeners, certain items of make-up and tampons were requested for their personal hygiene kits. They also requested that bikini underwear be added to the supply of men's boxer shorts.

Most of them were more used to working with men than with women in their various professions, so there was no feeling of awkwardness here at NASA.

Yet some of the men who had been with the program over the years admitted they had doubts at first. "We all wondered what changes it would make and whether or not the women could cut it," said one.

Apollo veteran Alan Bean, who was responsible for training when they first joined the program, was not at all happy with the idea of women astronauts. Later, he changed his mind. As scientists, they had had more computer training than most of the old-timers. They were used to solving problems from an analytical point of view.

Bean admitted, "At first I imagined they were just individuals trying to do a man's job. I was proven wrong. . . . Females intuitively understand astronaut skills. They perform the mental and physical tasks as well as men."

"We all knew it was coming," said Bob Crippin, pilot of the first Shuttle flight. "The only commotion I can remember around here was building a ladies' room into the gym."

The hardest adjustment for some of the women was starting all over with basics in other fields. Engineers were assigned research in physiology. Doctors studied astronomy, and when they were just about feeling competent in one field, jobs were shuffled.

No one complained, but pilot astronaut Lieutenant Commander Robert "Hoot" Gibson, who later married Dr. Seddon, says, "Rhea gets a little bit frustrated occasionally. She's a very accomplished person in her field. She's done some hard work and put in a lot of years to be a tremendous surgeon, and then we brought her down here and she didn't know anything. I know what it's like because I was an experienced test pilot, and when I came here I didn't know anything about rocket ships. It means starting all over."

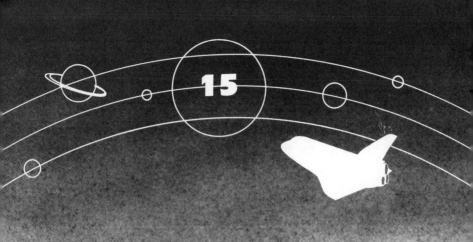

SIMULATING
THE MISSION

Training for men and women specialists is the same—intense. Whether it be an astronaut candidate still under evaluation, or a member of the astronaut corps waiting to be assigned a flight, or a crew member of an upcoming mission, an astronaut is always in training.

The first-year program breaks down into a three-part project. The first phase involves about 140 hours of classroom work that covers the spacecraft generally. There are lectures on the physics of the Shuttle; why it was designed with such stubby sweptback wings and tall tail section. Any normal aircraft designed to cruise in Earth's atmosphere with a cushion of air under its wings would have those wings ripped off in the first fiery minute of launch. The tail section gives the Shuttle stability when heading toward home.

The development of the heat shield and wing coating is described. Dozens of products were tested for their protective qualities, lightness of weight, and ability to be applied and replaced easily. The astronauts are beginning to realize what a remarkable piece of machinery they will be responsible for and how many people have had a hand in its development.

The power mechanisms of the craft are explained, from the tremendous rocket engines at liftoff to the more moderate thrusters that maneuver the Shuttle in space. Using liquid fuel under high pressure is a lot different than filling an ordinary gas tank.

The environmental systems are reviewed: how the air is kept fresh for breathing, how waste is disposed of, how the galley works.

The function of communication and control systems is covered in detail. Pictures of electrical wiring circuits begin to appear in the individuals' sleep as well as on the classroom blackboard. Repetition is the order of the day. They are becoming an expert repair crew, trained to cope with every imaginable emergency.

Orbital mechanics is on the agenda: how to control pitch and roll and speed when flashing around the Earth at 17,000 miles per hour with no brakes except a reverse thruster to slow the craft. It means backing into a precise position to adjust speed. Celestial navigation and space history are all subjects to be studied.

The second part of the classroom work includes training in engineering, astronomy, geology, and the life sciences. Every one of these subjects could be a full university major. In some cases the critical information needed for astronaut training exceeds what is expected for a Ph.D. This is what is meant by being a generalist. This is the kind of person NASA was searching for, a scientist who could expand his or her narrow expertise to new fields.

Although the fleet of Shuttles is always several hundred miles from Houston, the astronauts receive firsthand training in some very sophisticated copycat mock-ups at the Johnson Space Center. At the far end of the complex group of buildings is a very large structure the size of a football field and several stories high. Visitors are allowed in one section. The rest is off-limits unless you're scheduled for space flight in the near future.

At first glance it looks as if the Shuttle had had a serious breakup in landing. The cockpit stands by itself on one side of the room, reached by a ladder. The cargo bay is held in place on a cradle in another area. Way at the back you can see a kind of disjointed crane where the astronauts can practice retrieving satellites with the Remote Manipulator Arm.

This is only one place where they work at banks of controls simulating exact procedures in outer space, but it is the most complete. Suddenly classroom diagrams come to life. Everyone gets to stand in the cockpit of the craft and handle controls, scientists as well as pilots. In emergencies, every crew member is supposed to be replaceable. They must all learn each other's jobs.

Some of the astronauts have been asked if there was any competition among them to see who could acquire the best "grades." No one admitted there was any. "It's just sort of competing with ourselves to absorb as much information as quickly as possible." Because it is so very important to a team of astronauts to be able to depend on each other in the event of an emergency, it seems that even in training there is a sense of camaraderie rather than competition.

However, some of the old-timers admit that just before flight assignments are about to be posted, there is a certain tenseness in the air. A chance to fly in space is the goal of every astronaut. When they've trained months for this opportunity, there's bound to be disappointment if they are passed by. But with the present number of Shuttle flights planned for the future, all are bound to have a turn. Looking on the bright side, they realize that what one flight crew learns on a current mission makes the next flight safer for those who follow.

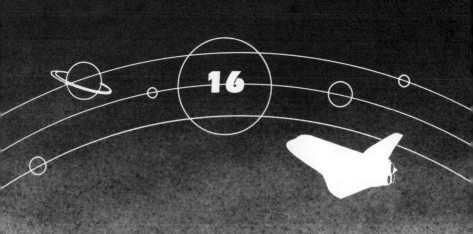

SURVIVAL
TRAINING

There was a lot the class of '78 had to go through before they were ready for their turn in space. The most exciting, or most frightening, was yet to come. Orientation to flight training was next on the schedule.

The new class of astronauts started at once going up as back-seat drivers in Air Force T-38 jet planes. Even those pilots like Shannon Lucid, with several hundred hours of flight time, had never experienced the "g" forces of such high-powered aircraft.

The T-38 is a two-seated trainer with dual controls. Instead of intimidating the new recruits, there was a clamor from passengers to take a turn as pilot. Permission was denied.

This jet trainer gave the astronauts a chance to learn all the rear-seat procedures, the importance of having a second pair of eyes reporting on performance readings, and handling communication and flight planning.

They were also introduced to a larger plane, the K-135, affectionately called the "vomit comet." During training, the plane heads almost straight toward the stratosphere, and at the top of the ascent makes a sharp curve for Earth. It's a bit like being at the end of a crack-the-whip line. The maneuver picks your feet off the floor for 30 seconds of weightlessness. The inside of the cabin is padded to ease the fall back to the world of gravity.

"It's a little different," says Judy Resnik. Quite an understatement. But the first six women astronauts to go through the training had no problems. Pictures of them taking swan dives and "swimming in space" shows them grinning like kids on a roller coaster ride.

Another first-year event is the Air Force Survival Course. This takes place on two locations, at the Homestead Air Force Base in Florida and the Vance Air Force Base near Enid, Oklahoma. "The purpose of the course is to prepare the trainees for proper

Ride walking away from a T-38 aircraft following a flight in the jet during her training as a mission specialist.

measures to take in the event of ejection from an aircraft, including the actual departure from the plane, the parachute drop and subsequent survival measures, over land or water," obviously not intended for outer-space survival.

Judy Resnik describes it in her matter-of-fact way, as if she had been sailing over water in a parachute as often as she'd been driving to work every day.

"You're in your flight equipment, and they hook you to an open parachute. They tow you off the deck of a stationary boat with a powerboat, so you end up about 500 feet in the air. Then they give you a signal to let go. The next minute or so is rather busy as you struggle out of your harness, inflate the rubber raft you're carrying, and set off flares for rescue."

Astronaut Ride gets ready to leave the ground, as she takes part in a parasail training exercise during a survival school. A pickup truck will move forward to cause Ride to ride from the ground, simulating a parachute glide.

She says this without a grin or a shudder, just routine in the life of an astronaut. The new class is proving itself unflappable. They are gaining special respect. They can cut it.

As soon as they were through with these tests, they were ready for the land training, off by plane to Oklahoma. First they were hung up in chute gear for short periods of time to get used to the feeling of being suspended in a parachute. Then they were pulled aloft attached to a parasail by a pickup truck, which again gave them the sensation of dropping from a high altitude. Sometimes those landings were harder than a fall from a plane. There were a few bruises, but no complaints.

There was also a diabolical gadget resembling a chair on rails. The astronauts lined up in groups of ten. Each one had a turn at being strapped in and waiting for the countdown. At a given signal the seat suddenly jerks and shoots straight up as if the occupant were being blasted out of a plane in ejection gear.

The rest of the survival training was directly related to the Shuttle. Obviously, the only time the crew can evacuate the craft is on launch and during descent, shortly before a normal landing. It is hard to imagine that such procedures would be required, but plans have been drawn up for all contingencies.

There's always a possibility that something could go wrong with the firing mechanisms while the Shuttle is still on the launch pad. If an abort is necessary before the solid rocket booster ignites, the access arm of the fixed service structure will

Some of the astronaut candidates who attended survival school in 1978. The overall course was designed to prepare the trainees with proper measures to take in the event of ejection from an aircraft over land.

move back into position so that the crew can exit through the hatch. Speed is important. There would be no time to take the elevator down. Any emergency would probably involve the volatile firing mechanism of the Shuttle.

The fastest way out is by way of slide wires. Five such wires extend from the service structure to the entrance of an underground bunker 1,200 feet away. There is a steel basket on each exit wire. Each of the five baskets can hold two people. The crew can slide down the wires to the bunker in about 35 seconds, 35 seconds to safety.

A pad abort is possible any time before the solid boosters ignite, but once these have been fired, there's no immediate turning back. The Shuttle is committed to at least a partial flight. Three alternative landing sites are available. The closest one is obviously at the Cape within sight of the launch tower, but with any altitude at all, considering the speed the Shuttle attains from the booster rockets, the pilot could probably make an emergency landing at the U.S. Naval Air Station in Rota, Spain. Sophisticated communications systems are set up there and chase planes are on hand to guide a ship down.

Edwards Air Force Base would be on the far range of the Shuttle path, but a familiar home base to touch down on if necessary.

Science fiction writers have often dreamed up the nightmarish story of astronauts being marooned in space. This is extremely unlikely with the Shuttle. Normally both orbital maneuvering system (OMS) engines fire for the slowdown and descent. If one fails, the other can function for the return. In the unlikely event that both are out of commission, there are still the weaker rockets that normally change the position of the Shuttle outside the limits of gravity. These would have to be fired for a longer push to head the Shuttle home, but computers, ground crews, and Shuttle pilots have practiced these maneuvers just in case they'd ever be needed.

If the worst happens and the Shuttle remains in orbit in spite of all other efforts, there's the possi-

Ride preparing for a simulated ejection during a training exercise.

In position in an aircraft-type seat just prior to "ejection" in an exercise that recreates the "feel" of ejection from an aircraft. The seat suddenly jerks and moves rapidly in an upward direction to simulate the experience.

bility of sending up another ship to take them home. This of course was not possible when the class of '78 astronauts was in training, because the Columbia was the only space vehicle in service at the time, but with a fleet of four orbiters planned for the future, they were put through the ultimate escape plan.

Seddon, Sullivan, Fisher, Ride, Lucid, and Resnik are briefed during training exercises at a survival school.

Several NASA astronaut candidates prepare to take part in a water-survival training exercise in 1978. Rhea Seddon is in the center, Sally Ride is at far left.

There are never more than two spacesuits aboard the Shuttle. They are bulky equipment and are used only for work outside the craft. In an emergency the crew would have to use rescue balls, those 30-inch-diameter fabric spheres that can be filled with enough lifesaving oxygen to keep a person alive during transfer. The two astronauts assigned to the bulky spacesuits would be responsible for attaching a line to the ball and delivering it to the rescue ship.

It is a frightening thought, but any astronaut who has passed the tests so far has proven to have bravery and faith in the safety of space flight. A lot can go wrong, but as scientists, they must consider the mathematical probabilities. Logically considering dangers ahead of time helps lessen panic if the moment should come.

All have had the experience of being zipped into these tiny rescue balls. Anyone having an acute case of claustrophobia has been eliminated. It's a reassuring thought that such equipment has been provided.

There is one other time these "personal rescue enclosures" might be put to use. If a toxic gas should contaminate the air of the cabin, the crew could crawl into the balloons or don spacesuits while the Shuttle is depressurized and the poison gas vented.

If a crew should have to make an emergency or abnormal landing, caused, for example, by a crippled landing gear, there are procedures on how to get out of the Shuttle as quickly as possible. Parachutes are useless. The Shuttle approaches land too fast and at too sharp an angle. Exit would be on the ground.

When the hatch is open there is a bar that can be swung out, which gives a handhold for jumping down to the ground. If the hatch sticks, a left-hand overhead window above the pilot's seat can be removed. Remembering that the body of the Shuttle is extremely hot, an insulated panel can be unrolled over the side of the plane. A rope, such as a mountain climber uses to rappel down a cliff at a controlled speed, is provided.

Safety precautions also include first aid medical training. Obviously, it would be ideal to have someone like Dr. Anna Fisher, trained as an emergency medic, aboard each time, but, even without her, every crew member is capable of handling injuries until the Shuttle is back on Earth. The Shuttle's medical kit includes everything from Band-Aids to a respirator and pills for various complaints.

One problem that has affected some astronauts in the past has been called space adaption syndrome, a tendency to feel nauseated in zero gravity. A type of medicated Band-Aid can be attached behind the ear of an astronaut. The medicine is absorbed slowly through the skin at a rate to halt the symptoms of nausea but not to affect the alertness of an astronaut. Before heading for space, the astronauts' systems are tested for certain doses. It isn't helpful to have a sleepy mission specialist fumbling with experiments. Their responses are monitored at all times.

Here Ride is suspended for a short time in abbreviated parachute gear during a training exercise. She can get used to the feel of being suspended in a parachute.

Wearing a parachute harness and complete ejection gear, Ride is again suspended. Shannon Lucid is in the background.

Ride drops to the ground.

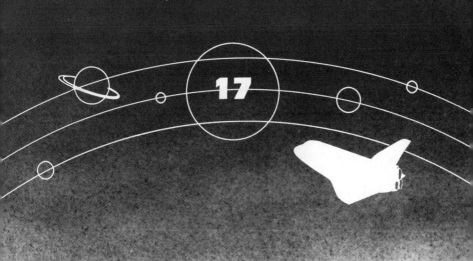

SUITING UP

After the rugged orientation program was over, more specific jobs were assigned. Anna Fisher was surprised to find herself under water for the first few months—not every hour of the day, but enough to make her wonder if she wasn't being trained to explore the sea bottom rather than outer space.

Actually the tank she was in had been carefully designed to fake the conditions an astronaut would feel in zero gravity. It is possible, with just the right balance of weight and buoyancy, to glide around in the water as you would in the nothingness of space. True, water acts as a slight drag. There will be none in space, but this is as close a feeling of weightlessness as is possible on Earth.

Anna had already passed tests as a scuba diver, but this didn't prepare her for the work she was expected to do in a bulky diving suit. The suit is much like the EMU (Extravehicular Mobility Unity) garment meant for space walks. Even the helmet and backpack are designed so the diver has the same angle of vision and mobility and balance.

The big NBS (Neutral Buoyancy Simulator) tank is located at the Marshall Space Center in Huntsville, Alabama. It is 75 feet wide and 50 feet deep, filled with 1.3 million gallons of see-through clear water. A smaller tank is located at the Johnson Center. On this day Anna was scheduled to test how well a person could use tools for specific jobs in water and space.

A mock-up of a space platform with a solar array system, which in space would be the battery pack energized by the sun, was already in place at the bottom of the tank. Anna was given a dry run of just what she was expected to do: remove the whole pack, all 900 pounds of it, which in water or space weighs nothing.

This would involve opening a pair of latches, removing a set of slide pins, and reassembling the pieces. When that was done, she was to head for the "phone booth," a boxed section with mock electric boxes. Connections had to be made on seven wires, ranging in thickness from fine to the thickness of a thumb.

Another astronaut in space gear would be in the water with her, and for the safety of both of them, two scuba divers are there if either of them get tangled in the equipment.

It takes a bit of doing just to get into the diving gear. Anna starts by putting on pants, then bending over to dive into the top and cram her head through the neck ring. Inside the suit, straps have been tightened to adjust the fit to her smaller size. Still, she looks like a small hippo with pleated knees.

She carefully backs into a boxlike cradle with forward-jutting arms. In a moment a crane lifts the whole apparatus high in the air, then gently lowers it into the tank. Clear water swirls over her face plate while television cameras record every movement.

A complete life-support system takes care of Anna's air supply, and she can communicate both with her partner and with the "ground crew." A metal rack across the chest plate lets her hang tools that might float out of her reach.

The gloves she wears were made as flexible as possible after months of research, but they are still clumsy. The first thing she must do is find a foot or handhold to keep herself in position for her job. Otherwise, she keeps floating away. This is a problem astronauts have found in space.

"If you can do it in the water tank, you can do it in zero gravity," said Jack Lousma, commander of the second Skylab crew. "It's a great training and development tool."

When he was up in space, he beamed down the enthusiastic message, "It's just like the tank in Huntsville, only deeper."

Anna continues to work slowly, patiently. It is tiring work. At the end of two hours she is ready to be hoisted to the surface again.

Both astronauts are questioned on how the job can be made easier. Could tools be improved? Should extra handholds be added to the equipment? Every comment is noted, and then it's back to the tank for another exercise.

The real outfit for space walks is a close copy of the tank suit. It is a monstrously heavy garment on Earth when attached to the portable life-support system (PLSS) backpack. Yet this is a great improvement over the less flexible model Astronaut Edward H. White wore in 1965 on America's first space walk.

Beneath the suit a cooling and ventilation garment is worn, made of spandex mesh with plastic tubing woven into the mesh. With the extremes of hot and cold in outer space, this is a lifesaving part of the suit.

The space suit, more properly referred to as the extravehicular mobility unit, or EMU, is made in several standard sizes. Inside the suit are straps that can be adjusted for an acceptable fit.

The EMU is made in three parts. The upper torso chest portion is rigid with aluminum supports. A chest-mounted microcomputer gives an astronaut an up-to-date reading on the supply of oxygen and battery power. Other instruments are mounted here. With a push of a button the wearer can control temperature, fan, radio, and rate of oxygen intake.

Trousers come with boots attached. A connecting ring around the waist joins the two parts. Shoulder, elbow, and knee joints resemble a pleated bellows, so that as one side contracts the other expands, keeping the interior volume, and hence pressure, constant.

Gloves made in fifteen different sizes have molded finger caps so that the wearer has a certain amount of feeling for delicate jobs.

The helmet is similar to that worn by the astronauts who landed on the moon. Inside the plastic bubble helmet there are two microphones and a set of earphones. A gold-plated visor protects the eyes from ultraviolet radiation and from micrometeoroids.

Old suits took more than an hour to put on and "a dresser" was required to check zip locks and hose connections. With the new design a space walker can dress and undress in a matter of minutes. However, preparation starts at least two hours before final exit into space.

The cabin atmosphere of the Shuttle is 79 percent nitrogen and 21 percent oxygen and is kept constantly at a slightly higher pressure than is used inside the suit. A crew member would suffer from the bends if he or she were to go directly into the pure oxygen pressure-reduced environment of the space suit. The nitrogen gas dissolved in the blood would bubble out, causing painful pressure around joints.

About two hours before dressing for space, astronauts start breathing pure oxygen from a face mask. This slowly "washes" nitrogen from their bodies.

Space workers must travel through an airlock without depressurizing the entire crew compartment.

For some work in space a power unit or Manned Maneuvering Unit (MMU) is added to the backpack. It looks a lot like the cradle Anna Fisher used in the water tank. Arms jut forward that hold the controls. Twenty-four jets powered by pressurized nitrogen are capable of accelerating to speeds of 66 feet (19 meters) per second. However, most tasks are performed in much slower movements, about the speed you'd be going up an escalator.

Yet these figures are all relative, as the free-flying astronauts are already traveling at 17,500 miles per hour as they circle the Earth once every 90 minutes. There is no sensation of speed. It is as if they were drifting weightlessly in the water tank at Huntsville.

That may seem strange, but think of a fly inside of a car that is going 50 miles an hour. It can't really be said the fly itself is traveling at that speed, yet it travels that far.

These MMU units were first used in February 1984 by astronauts Bruce McCandless and Robert Stewart. It was the first time a human, without being attached by tether to a spaceship, had become a satellite himself.

Every astronaut practices the procedures for work outside of the Shuttle, even if the mission does not schedule such a procedure. It's sort of a lifeboat drill.

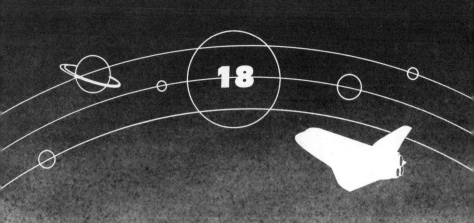

WHERE THEY
HANG THE BIRD

While Anna Fisher was floating in the neutral
buoyancy tank, Judy Resnik and Sally Ride were
working in Toronto, Canada with the engineers of
SPAR Aerospace Ltd. It was here the scientists
developed the remote manipulator system, known
briefly as RMS, which Sally Ride and John Fabian
used to retrieve a piece of equipment on the STS 7
flight.

They practiced until they were able to pick up small delicate instruments as well as large cumbersome objects. "It got to be as natural as using tweezers on a noodle," Sally laughs. "I began to think that all there was to being an astronaut was launching an arm."

Everybody was doing her own thing. Shannon Lucid spent time in California working on landing procedures. Kathy Sullivan worked on computer calculations for alternative landing sites. Training increasingly became a matter of self-discipline.

"Your job description is generally a one-liner," Kathy Sullivan said. "'Why don't you go work at the Cape?' Nobody sits on you to make sure you work from eight to four. It's 'Get the job done.'"

You do it, they all say, because you are continually challenged, continually learning—something that is very important to these extraordinary people.

Every one of the astronauts is expected to keep up with his or her own specialty. It may be continuing research through a university or just hours going over technical papers published by others.

To sharpen their medical skills both Anna and Rhea rode in rescue helicopters. "In training exercises," Dr. Seddon says, "we try to simulate situations that could actually happen. We 'rescue' uniformed dummies, perform emergency procedures on them in shaky, noisy helicopters, and then get them to our back-up trauma centers."

The astronauts are being trained in how to give emergency care at launchings and landings.

By the time Bonnie Dunbar and Mary Cleave joined the astronaut corps in 1980, the groundwork had been laid. No one gave a second glance to Mary, with her waist-length hair streaming out behind her as she jogged between buildings at the Space Center.

Both women came into the program with specialties of their own. Mary Cleave was a sanitary engineer with fancy credentials from her work with micro-organisms, looking toward the future when a closed-loop recycle system would be a necessity in a space station. Her first job was to work on the space toilet of the Shuttle.

"Right now I'm working at SAIL," she explains, which is the Shuttle Avionics Integration Lab. "The lab runs 24 hours a day, seven days a week. So one week I could be going to work at seven in the morning, getting off about four or five. Next week I could get the swing shift or else I can get graveyard, just like any factory job. Like on my last shift, I was testing ascent procedures."

Bonnie Dunbar was already well acquainted with NASA, having been in on the beginning of the heat shield testing for the Shuttle. She had gotten used to some pretty incredible facts and figures about space travel, but the big surprises were all at the Cape. That is where tiny mortals control giant machines, where they hang the "bird," fuel it, test cargo packages, where they put it all together.

When approaching from the west, Cape Canaveral is a desolate-looking landscape, at first glance, water-pocked swampland and palmetto brush. Yet the Space Center, which is surrounded by the Merritt Island National Wildlife Refuge, covering 140,000 acres of land and water, protects more endangered species of birds, mammals, and reptiles than any other area of the continental United States. Just don't step too far off cleared tracks, because this wildlife also includes several kinds of poisonous snakes. Somehow, life seems to have sorted itself out satisfactorily. The public comes to look only; the military and space complex comes to work; the wildlife is there to make their home, and each has laid out privacy markers of its own.

The string-straight horizon toward the ocean is broken by the imposing sight of a 50-story building, the Vehicle Assembly Building, and the towering scaffolds of the launching pads. The headquarters of the Kennedy Space Center is a long factory-like building where the management offices are located and where the several thousand contractor and support personnel are housed. Altogether some 13,000 people are employed in the complex, making it a small town all by itself.

The Central Instrumentation Facility is filled with space-age computers, and the huge dish-shaped radio antenna is the communications link by satellite between the Kennedy Space Center, Mission Control in Houston, and other NASA centers.

There is a Flight Crew Training Building where simulated problems can be fed into computers, and there is the area where the parachutes for the fuel tanks are cleaned, inspected, and repackaged.

The Orbiter Processing Facility is essentially a

hangar with two high bays, in which orbiters, two at a time, can undergo "safing" and servicing after landing. The orbiter is technically not a Shuttle until its fuel tanks are attached, but it is here that propellant feedlines are drained and cleaned. Flight and landing systems are refurbished, returned payloads are removed, and everything is set in motion for the next mission.

Dominating the entire landscape is the 525-foot-tall Vehicle Assembly Building. It covers eight acres of ground, and with an inside volume of 129 million cubic feet, it is one of the world's largest enclosed structures. Under certain conditions, it develops weather all its own. Changing climate can cause updrafts and even an occasional fog bank to form, something to guard against.

The orbiter ready for processing is towed through the towering doors. It is now rotated by huge cranes to a vertical position, lifted 190 feet above the floor, then swung ever so gently over a large structural beam and lowered to the deck of the mobile launcher platform.

The twin solid-rocket boosters are erected on the platform first; the 15-story-tall external belly tank is added. Here the whole Shuttle is assembled while standing on its tail.

The next procedure is to move the unwieldy structure three and a half miles away to the launch pad. The Crawler Transporter is capable of lifting and carrying 14,500,000 pounds. Each Transporter is about half the size of a soccer field and weighs about six million pounds not loaded.

It is powered by two diesel electric generators.

Ride is seated at a capsule communicator console in the mission operations control room of the Johnson Space Center's mission control center.

The generators, in turn, power electric motors which turn the huge army tank-like treads. Each cleat of the crawler weighs a ton, and a very special runway had to be constructed that would withstand tremendous pressure without caving in or buckling.

A hydraulic system can vary the Transporter's height at either or both ends so that when it slowly crawls up the incline to the launch pad, the Shuttle remains firmly level in an upright position. One man does the driving, but there is a crew of 26 trained engineers aboard to check every procedure along the way. Top speed when loaded is about one mile an hour.

Bonnie was there to witness these exciting steps several times, as she inspects the Shuttles for burn damage before being reserviced for flight.

She looks longingly at the spacecraft. "I'm not trying to overcompensate for being a woman," Dunbar insists, "but with enough flying time, who knows? One of us could get to command a mission sometimes. Then we'll get our chance to fly that beautiful Shuttle."

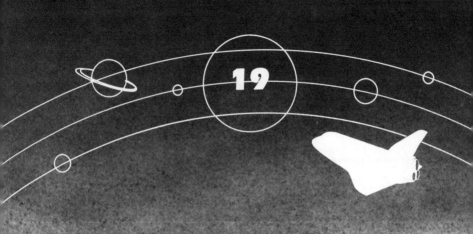

WHOSE TURN
NEXT?

What do these superpowered women do in their down-to-earth off time? Just about the same things their neighbors do. It's true that all of them are sports oriented, either as a natural hobby they've always enjoyed, or as a more recent activity to keep in shape physically.

The Fishers are likely to find a remote spot backpacking. Kathy Sullivan loves to sail, and she's proved herself a winning skipper. But at the moment she's without a boat of her own. Not enough time for one. Mary Cleave gets back to Utah every now and then to visit the old gang and do some skiing, but she finds it hard to fit the role of celebrity.

"It has its disadvantages," she says. She was in the grocery store shopping when she noticed there were stares. "First they asked me if they hadn't seen my picture. Was I an astronaut? Then they'd start looking over every single thing in my shopping cart. They'd ask me why I was buying junk food. You just can't be perfect."

There's an occasional backyard barbecue in the Houston area when a NASA group gets together. Sally Ride met her husband Steven Hawley in 1978 while they were both in training for the space program. Steven is a graduate of the University of California where he earned a Ph.D. in astronomy, Sally's field of interest too.

They were married July 24, 1982. The bride wore Levis and a Rugby shirt and flew her own plane to the wedding in her husband's hometown in Kansas. They have decided not to have children of their own.

The first time Sally babysat for a friend's family, her father recalls, the children refused to eat the sandwiches she prepared because she put the peanut butter and jelly on in the wrong order. Without arguing, she threw the sandwiches out, made another batch, and never ever again babysat with anybody's children.

Two other women astronauts, Rhea Seddon and

Anna Fisher, have decided to combine motherhood and space travel. Rhea married astronaut pilot Lieutenant Commander Robert Gibson. Their son Paul Seddon Gibson was born in 1982, and the Fisher's daughter, Kirstin Ann, arrived a year later. Motherhood is old hat for Shannon Lucid, whose kids were already of school age when she was selected as an astronaut.

It was clear that each of the women was being given plenty of responsibility, and it was very noticeable that Sally Ride was destined to do more than arm work with the remote manipulator system. She was given the chance to be a capcom, or capsule communicator, the only link between the astronauts in space and the officials on the ground, what TV commentators have called "the voice of Mission Control."

In November 1981, during the second Shuttle flight, it was Sally who broke the news to Joe Engle and Dick Truly that their mission had been cut short because of the loss of a power-producing cell.

During the third Shuttle flight Ride again was at Mission Control when the robot arm was being tested. A broken camera on the arm threatened to cancel the experiment. She came up with a solution to the problem which salvaged that portion of the work.

On the same flight the astronauts were involved in taking blood samples of each other and analyzing them. Suddenly one of the astronauts appeared on the television screen hanging upside down from Columbia's ceiling.

Touring the facility where Space Shuttle **Columbia** was assembled.

Veering from her businesslike clipped, no-nonsense communications, Ride radioed, "Hey, is that the vampire to go with the red blood cells?"

Rumors had been spreading that one of the eight women would soon be scheduled for a future flight. It's been said that the biggest mystery around is how flight crews are chosen, although it is assumed that George Abbey, director of flight operations, and John Young, the chief of the astronaut office and commander of the first Shuttle flight, make the final decision.

Abbey, who wears his military crew cut at practically scalp level, has the unenviable position of selecting each flight commander, who in turn has an opportunity to make suggestions for crew members.

The idea is to find the most experienced person for the job at hand. When the announcement was made that Sally Ride was to be the first woman from the United States in space, a qualifying statement was also issued.

"Since the women are there because of their skills, Dr. Ride's selection for STS-7 doesn't imply that she is the best of the women astronauts. Her skills were most needed on this particular mission."

Commander Robert Crippen gave his own reasons for seconding Sally's selection. "Sally is a very smart lady. She is smart in a special way. You get people who sit in the lab and think like Einstein, but they can't do anything with it. Now Sally can get everything she knows together and bring it to bear where you need it. . . . There's an awful lot to watch up there and we need a third pair of eyeballs."

There was very little jealousy with the selection; envy, yes. "Any one of us would like to swap places with Sally," Kathy Sullivan admits. "And yet being first brings with it an added load of responsibility. I don't know that any one of us can ever put all the skeptics to rest, and it's unfair that Sally should have that burden entirely on her shoulder," Kathy added thoughtfully.

"Sally was selected for this flight as testimony to her ability to perform on the job," said Mary Cleave. "She's going to blow everyone's socks off, because she's a real competent lady. There will be a bunch of little girls on this planet who will be looking at Sally and saying, 'Hey, if I want to be an astrophysicist, that's okay.' It gives girls of today options we didn't have when we were kids.''

Sally Ride has her own page in history, but there is plenty more to put on the record. During the next few months all eight of the women astronauts are scheduled for space flights.

Number two in line is Judith Resnik with a flight June 4, 1984. August 9 is the date of Rhea Seddon's trip. On August 30 records will be broken with two women in space at the same time, Sally Ride and Kathryn Sullivan. Kathy will be the first woman ever to don a spacesuit for work outside the Space Shuttle. Anna Fisher will be going September 28 and Shannon Lucid on October 24, followed the next year by Mary Cleave on February 1, 1985, and Bonnie Dunbar on September 20th.

SUGGESTED FURTHER READINGS

Bendick, Jeanne. *Space Travel*. New York: Franklin Watts, 1982.

Berger, Melvin. *Space Shots, Shuttles and Satellites*. New York: G. P. Putnam's Sons, 1983.

Hodgman, Ann, and Ruby Djabbaroff. *Skystars– The History of Women in Aviation*. New York: Atheneum, 1981.

O'Connor, Karen. *Sally Ride and the New Astronauts*. New York: Franklin Watts, 1983.

Pastor, Terry, illus. *Space Mission*. Boston: Little Brown, 1983.

Smith, Elizabeth Simpson. *Breakthrough—Women in Aviation*. New York: Walker and Co., 1981.

Vogt, Gregory. *The Space Shuttle—Projects for Young Scientists*. New York: Franklin Watts, 1983.

INDEX

Abbey, George, 55, 98, 153
Abrahamson, L.T. Gen. James, 41
Air Force Survival Course, 124
Anik satellite, 27
Antigravity pants, 41
Apollo, 12, 59, 103, 117

Bean, Alan, 117
Berry, Dr., 54
Bridges, Roy, 18

Cabin atmosphere, space shuttle, 141
Cape Canaveral, 39–40, 44, 145–46
Central Instrumentation Facility, 146
Challenger, 6, 13
Cleave, Mary, 90, 91–101, 145, 151, 154, 155
Coats, Lt. Com. Michael, 100–1
Collins, Michael, 59
Columbia, 26, 132, 153
Communication satellites, 26
Crawler Transporter, 147–48
Crippen, Com. Robert L., 6, 7, 19, 23, 31, 36–38, 39, 41, 43–44, 117, 154

Drew, Nancy, 48
Dunbar, Bonnie, 103–8, 145, 149, 155
Durante, Jimmy, 33

Edwards Air Force Base, 41, 129
Ehricke, Dr. Kraft, 107
EMU (Extravehicular Mobility Unity), 138, 140–41
Engle, Joe, 152
EVA (Extra Vehicular Activity), 80

Fabian, John, 6, 27, 33, 36
Fisher, Dr. Anna, 84, 85–89, 111, 113, 132, 135, 137–38, 139–40, 143, 144, 150, 152, 155
Fisher, Bill, 87–88, 150
Fisher, Kirstin Ann, 89, 150, 152
Flight Crew Training Building, 146
Foods, dehydrated or freeze-dried, 21

Gardner, Guy, 36
Gemini, 12, 103
Getaway Specials, 31–32
Gibson, Paul Seddon, 152
Gibson, Lt. Com. Robert "Hoot," 117–18, 152
Glenn, John, 20–21
"Glitch," 38

Hargadon, Fred, 53
Hartwell Laboratories, 106
Hauck, Com. Frederick H., 6, 7, 39, 48
Hawley, Steven, 151

Heinlein, Robert, 93
Homestead Air Force Base, 124
Huntoon, Dr. Carolyn, 55, 88
Hygiene kits, 25

International Women Pilots Association, 65–66

Johnson Space Center (Houston), 53, 107, 109–10, 112, 121

Kennedy Space Center, 146. *See also* Cape Canaveral
King, Billie Jean, 49
K-135 plane ("vomit comet"), 124

Lousma, Jack, 139
Lucid, Mike, 73, 75
Lucid, Shannon, 69–77, 111, 123–24, 132, 133, 136, 144, 152, 155

McCandless, Bruce, 142
McDonnell Douglas Aircraft Corporation, 33
Manned Maneuvering Unit (MMU), 142
Marble, Alice, 49
Marshall Space Center, 138
Meals, aboard the Shuttle, 20–23
Mercury, 12, 86, 103
Mission Control, 42, 146, 152
Mommaerts, Elizabeth, 50, 51
Mullane, Maj. Richard, 100–1

NASA, 8, 16, 27, 30, 33, 40, 43, 45, 53, 58, 59, 60, 61, 66, 67, 68, 81, 82, 87, 88, 95–96, 97, 101, 106, 107, 112, 115, 116, 146, 151
National Air and Space Museum, 59

NBS (Neutral Buoyancy Simulator), 138

Orbital maneuvering system (OMS), 42, 129
Orbiter Processing Facility, 146–47

Palapa B satellite, 31
Pauley, Jane, 48
Pleats, uniform, 8–10
Portable life-support system (PLSS) backpack, 140

Reagan, Ronald, 45
Remote manipulator system (RMS), 34–38, 143
Resnik, Judith, 56, 57–62, 111, 113, 124, 125–27, 132, 143, 155
Ride, Joyce, 45, 48
Ride, Karen, 48
Ride, Sally, 6, 19, 46, 47–55, 111, 113, 114, 116, 135, 143, 144, 148, 151, 153, 154–55
  STS-7 space flight, 7–45
  survival training, 126, 130, 131, 132, 133, 135, 136
Rockwell International, 106, 107

Seddon, Dr. Margaret Rhea, 63–68, 111, 113, 118, 132, 144, 151–52, 155
Shepard, Alan, 86
Shuttle Avionics Integration Lab, 145
Shuttle Pallet Satellite (SPAS), 35–36
Simulating the mission, 119–22
Skylab, 103, 139
Space-adaption syndrome, 19, 135
Space Cadet (Heinlein), 93
Space gear, 137–42

SPAR Aerospace Ltd., 143
Stewart, Robert, 142
STS-7 (Space
    Transportation—Flight
    7), 7–45, 143, 154
  bathroom facilities, 25–26
  blastoff, 7–17
  chores and routine in
    flight, 30–38
  control panels, 11–12
  crew, 6
  descent, 41–44
  hygiene kits, 25
  housekeeping chores, 19
  launch position, 11
  liftoff, 16
  meals aboard, 20–23
  RMS, 34–38
  sleeping aboard, 27–28, 29
  television pictures, 19–20
  water and electricity,
    24–25
  weather glitch, 39–45
  wings and rockets, 10
Sullivan, Kathryn, 78,
    79–83, 111, 113, 132, 144,
    150–51, 154, 155
Survival training, 123–36
  abort, 127–29
  first-year, 124–27
  related to the Shuttle,
    127–35
  safety precautions,
    133–35
  space adaption syndrome,
    135

Thagard, Dr. Norman, 7, 19,
    31, 36
T-38 aircraft, 124, 125
Truly, Dick, 152
Tyson, Molly, 51–52

U.S. Geological Survey, 82
U.S. Naval Air Station
    (Rota, Spain), 129

Utah Water Research
    Laboratory, 95

Vance Air Force Base, 124
Vehicle Assembly Building,
    146, 147

WCS (waste collection
    system), 26
Weather glitch, 39–45
Weightlessness, 18, 138
Wells, Oscar and Rachel, 69
White, Edward H., 140
Wilson, Gahan, 101
Women astronauts
  as candidates, 109–18
  off time activities, 150–55
  simulating the mission,
    119–22
  space gear, 137–42
  survival training, 123–36
  See also names of
    astronauts
Woods Hole Oceanographic
    Institute, 82

Young, John, 153

ABOUT THE AUTHOR

Mary Virginia Fox was born in Richmond, Virginia. She graduated from Northwestern University, as did her entire family for the past three generations. She is the author of many books for young people. She lives with her husband and three sons in Middleton, Wisconsin, where she spends most of her time writing and traveling.